Michael Müller

Prayer, the key of salvation

Michael Müller

Prayer, the key of salvation

ISBN/EAN: 9783337278670

Printed in Europe, USA, Canada, Australia, Japan

Cover: Foto ©Lupo / pixelio.de

More available books at **www.hansebooks.com**

PRAYER

THE

KEY OF SALVATION.

BY

MICHAEL MÜLLER, C. SS. R.

Priest of the Congregation of the Most Holy Redeemer.

"Amen, amen I say to you: If you ask the Father anything in My name, He will give it you. Hitherto you have not asked anything in My name. Ask, and you shall receive; that your joy may be full."—JOHN xvi., 23, 24.

BALTIMORE:

KELLY AND PIET,

174 Baltimore Street.

1868.

PREFACE.

"THE Jews, therefore, murmured at Him, because He had said: I am the living bread which came down from heaven." (John vi. 41.) "This murmuring at the doctrine of our Lord Jesus Christ is," says St. Cyrillus, "the inheritance which was bequeathed to the Jews by their forefathers, who lived at the time of Moses." Would to God that this inheritance had been transmitted to the Jews only; but, alas! there is no class of men which is free from such murmurers. Our Lord's doctrine is murmured at by infidels when they hear Him say: "He that believeth not shall be condemned" (Mark xvi. 16) . . . . "because he believeth not in the name of the only begotten Son of God." (John iii. 18.) The doctrine of our Lord is murmured at by Protestants, when He declares: "Not every one that saith to Me, Lord, Lord, shall enter into the kingdom of heaven, but he that doth the will of My Father who is in Heaven, he shall enter into the kingdom of heaven." (Matt. vii. 21.) The will of God has not been taught by Luther, or Calvin, or Henry VIII., or John Wesley, or by another man who invented certain doctrines, and founded a sect according to his own private notions, but it has been taught by Me, the Son of God, Who have charged Peter and his lawful successors to do the same. Upon him I have built My Church; to him and his lawful successors I have said: "He who heareth you heareth Me, and he that despiseth you despiseth Me, and he who despiseth Me despiseth Him that sent Me." One who does not do this will be condemned. "There is a way (the Protestant religion) that seemeth to a man right, and the ends therefore lead to death." (Prov. xvi. 25.) Sinners murmur when our Blessed Saviour preaches: "I say to you that unless you shall do penance, you shall all likewise perish." (Luke xiii. 3.) The rich also complain, when He threatens "Woe to you that are rich, for you have your consolation." (Luke vi. 24.) The poor are dissatisfied when He teaches: "Blessed are the poor in spirit." (Math. v. 3.) The learned reject His doctrine when he warns: "Amen I say to you: unless you be converted and become as little children, you shall not enter into the kingdom of heaven." (Math. xviii. 3.) The young are displeased when He exclaims: "Woe to you that now laugh, for you shall mourn and weep." (Luke vi. 25.) Those who are tempted or afflicted, murmur when He exhorts them by His words and example: "Not my will but Thine be done." (Luke xxii. 42.) The lukewarm are displeased when He tells them: "Because thou art lukewarm, and neither cold nor hot, I will begin to vomit thee out of My mouth." (Apoc. iii. 16.) Finally, the greater part of men murmur at our Lord, when He teaches: "The kingdom of heaven suffereth violence and the violent bear it away." (Matt. xi. 12.) They complain with the unfaithful disciples of our Lord, "these are hard sayings who can hear them." (John vi. 61.)

There are still many, it is true, who will say with St. Peter and the other Apostles: "Lord, to whom shall we go? Thou hast the words of eternal life, and we have believed and have known that Thou art Christ the Son of God." (John vi. 69, 70.) But how many, even among these, will murmur, not indeed at Christ's doctrine, but at heretics, unbelievers and great sinners? How many are there who, like the Apostles, not knowing of what spirit they are, wish that fire should come down from heaven to consume them (Luke ix. 54, 55), for not believing, in spite of so many miracles and evident proofs, confirming the truth of the Catholic religion? To all these our Lord answers with divine sweetness: "Murmur not among yourselves: no man can come to Me, except the Father, who hath sent Me, draw him." (John vi. 44.) As to all those of you, He means to say, who believe in Me and live up to My doctrine, you ought not to murmur at infidels, heretics or nominal Christians, on account of their infidelity, false belief or bad life, but

1*

you should remember that faith, especially practical faith, is a supernatural gift of God, and that no one can have true faith in Him unless it is granted by My heavenly Father. Since they are not as yet drawn by the Father, you should not feel indignant or treat them with severity, but rather pray to the Father that He may draw them sweetly, but powerfully, by enlightening their understanding to know the true faith, and by exciting their will to embrace it in practice, and thus they will be united with you in the same religion.

But as to you who do not believe My doctrine, or believe only a part of it, or live not according to it, neither ought you to murmur at Me and My doctrine or at those who believe truly in Me, because My Father has drawn them. Pray you, too, to My Father that He may draw you also, by removing from your understanding the darkness which prevents you from knowing My Church and the truths she teaches. Pray that He may remove from your heart the coldness and indifference which prevents you from loving the truth, and from your will the reluctance and resistance which prevents you from embracing it. For this purpose, you should often say to God in all sincerity: "Our Father, who art in heaven, if there are still more truths which I must know and practise, in order to be saved, I beseech Thee, for the sake of Jesus Christ, permit me to know them in whatever way it pleaseth Thee to manifest them to me. Give me a good will that I may embrace them and practise faithfully what they command, until the end of my life." If you pray perseveringly, in this manner, rest assured that you also will be drawn by My Father, to live and die with My true followers in the same faith. All your unjust murmurs and complaints would soon be changed into joy, as I have promised when I said: "Ask and you shall receive, that your joy may be full," (John xvi. 24), for My Father "is rich unto all that call upon Him," (Rom. x. 12) in My name, for the sake of which I will grant that life of which I have said: "I am come that they may have life, and have it more abundantly," (John x. 10), here by My exuberant grace and hereafter by My unspeakable glory.

This doctrine, of such vital importance for the salvation of mankind, is too seldom preached, little understood, and still less put in practice, "God thus permitting it," says St. Alphonsus, "in punishment for the sins of men."

"And now, brethren, as you are the ancients among the people of God, and their very soul resteth upon you, comfort their hearts by your speech" (Judith viii. 21), by explaining to them, as often and as plainly as possible, the great necessity of this doctrine on prayer, as well as the right manner of practising it, in order to derive therefrom all possible advantage.

In this book I have tried, my dear reader, to do this ; wherefore, I venture to assert that the reading of it will be more profitable to you than the perusal of any other book, for the more you read it the more you will find this assertion to be true. I pray you to read it again and again with great attention, not because it is my production, but because it is a means which God offers you to enable you to attain eternal salvation, thereby giving you to understand that He wishes you to be saved. When you have finished reading this book, induce as many of your friends as you can to read it also.

You must also thank the Lord for what He teaches you in this book, " for it is a great mercy," says St. Alphonsus, " when He gives the light and grace to pray and to understand the importance of prayer." "Ah, my dear brethren," wrote Pope Celestine to the Bishops of France, " let prayer never leave your hearts, and the grace and mercy of God will never leave your souls. Rest assured that the Lord will never withdraw from you, nor cease to enlighten, guide and protect you as long as you pray to Him. You complain of the difficulty of saving your souls in the midst of a corrupt world, in which you are exposed to so many dangers. Do you wish to escape them all and to fear none ? Arm yourselves with prayer. Prayer was the daily food and strength of the prophet ; it was his whole delight ; he understood but too well all its advantages."

PROTEST OF THE AUTHOR.

IN obedience to the decrees of Urban VIII. of holy memory, I protest that I do not intend to attribute any other than purely human authority to all the miracles, revelations, graces and incidents contained in this book; neither to the titles holy or blessed applied to the servants of God not yet canonized, except in cases where these have been confirmed by the Holy Roman Catholic Church and by the Holy Apostolic See, of whom I profess myself an obedient son; and, therefore, to their judgment I submit myself and whatever I have written in this book.

OBLATION.

MY Lord Jesus Christ, behold I offer Thee this little work in union with that unspeakable charity which moved Thee to say: " Whatsoever you ask the Father in My name, that will I do: that the Father may be glorified in the Son. If you ask Me anything in My name, that I will do." (John xiv. 13, 14.) I offer this book to Thee on the part of all Thy creatures, because it is Thine ineffable tenderness for them which caused Thee to make them so unlimited a promise, thereby to draw them to Thyself and to unite them to Thee eternally. Take this book, I beseech Thee, into Thy divine keeping, that it may glorify the omnipotence of Thy Father, Thy own infinite wisdom and the unspeakable love of the Holy Ghost. I offer it to Thee in fervent thanksgiving for all the graces which Thou hast bestowed or wilt bestow through this little work, even to the end of the world. Place it, I beseech Thee, upon Thy most merciful heart, that every word contained therein may be penetrated with Thy divine sweetness, and fertilized by the merits of Thy holy Life and of Thy Five Wounds. Consecrate, by an everlasting benediction, all that is said therein, that it may promote the salvation of those who read it with humble devotion. Inspire them with an irresistible desire of giving themselves up to prayer, that thus may be accomplished that exceedingly great desire of Thine of manifesting Thyself to them in all Thy eternal goodness and charity; take them, as it were, into Thy Divine Heart as into a safe harbor of salvation, and breathe into their souls Thy eternal Divine life and truth.

And as I am an utterly vile and unworthy creature, I offer Thee, in satisfaction for all my deficiencies and omissions, my blindness and ignorance, Thy own sweetest Heart, ever full of Divine thanksgiving and eternal beatitude.

Dear Mother Mary, do you also pray to your Divine Son for all those who may read this little book.

CONTENTS

Imprimatur...	2
Preface...	3
Protest of the Author.................................	9
Oblation...	10
CHAPTER I—On the Necessity of Prayer in General....	13
CHAPTER II—On the Necessity of Prayer for Sinners...	33
CHAPTER III—On the Necessity of Prayer for the Just	47
CHAPTER IV—On the Necessity of Prayer for Ecclesiastical Students..	69
CHAPTER V—On the Efficacy of the Prayer of the Just	117
CHAPTER VI—On the Conditions and Qualities of Prayer	140
I—The Object of our Prayer must be Lawful...	141
II—Our Prayer must be Humble..............	160
III—Our Prayer must be Fervent..............	165
IV—Our Prayer must be followed by Amendment of Life.................................	177

CHAPTER VI—v—Our Prayer must be United with Forgiveness of Injuries..................... 187

vi—Our Prayer must be United with Good Works............................ 194

vii—Our Prayer must be Confident...... 200

viii—Our Prayer must be Persevering.... 231

CHAPTER VII—How to Acquire the Spirit of Prayer... 239

CHAPTER VIII—Eulogium on Prayer......... 260

PRAYER—To Obtain the Grace of being Constant in Prayer..................................... 265

PRAYER—To be said every day, to obtain the Graces Necessary for Salvation............................. 267

PRAYER of Chlodwig, (Clovis,)........................... 270

PRAYER for Guidance into Truth.......................... 271

Ejaculation.. 272

TREATISE ON PRAYER.

CHAPTER I.

ON THE NECESSITY OF PRAYER IN GENERAL.

THERE is an important truth, of which thousands of men are ignorant; or, if they know it, they reflect upon it seldom and with little fruit. Yet, the knowledge of this truth is almost as necessary for those who have attained the age of reason, as it is for them to know that there is only one God in three Persons, and that the Second Person became man to redeem and save us. The importance and necessity of this great truth seem to be a mystery, not to heathens, Jews, and heretics only, but also to the greater part of Christians, nay, even to many of those who have especially consecrated themselves to God. We often hear in sermons and read in pious books of the necessity of avoiding bad company, of hating sin, of forgiving injuries, and of being reconciled with our enemies, but seldom are we taught this great truth; or, if it is sometimes spoken of, rarely is it done in a manner and with that interior conviction calculated to leave upon our minds and " hearts a convincing and lasting impression of its great importance and necessity. Now, this important truth is that, morally speaking, or according to the ordinary course of Divine Providence, man cannot be saved without prayer.

In order to understand this truth in its full extent, we must consider :

First. That man cannot be saved unless he will have done God's will.

Secondly. That man is unable to do God's will, unless he is assisted by Divine grace.

Thirdly. That man obtains this grace by prayer only ; that, consequently, man must pray in order to be saved.

First, I say, man cannot be saved unless he will have done God's will on earth. The Lord declared this will in express terms when He said to Adam : "And of the tree of knowledge of good and evil thou shalt not eat ; for in what day soever thou shalt eat of it, thou shalt die the death." (Gen ii., 17.) By this commandment, man was evidently given to understand that the continuation of his happiness for time and eternity, depended upon his obedience to the will of God. To be undisturbed by any irregular affections or disorderly passions and to perpetuate his happiness to his posterity, was entirely optional with him. If he made a right use of his liberty, by always following the law and will of God, if he bore unsullied the image and likeness of his Creator, as a true son of his Father, to Whom he owed filial affection as a good servant of his Master, Whom he was to fear and honor, as a brave soldier of his King, to Whom he owed fidelity, as a wise steward and administrator of the goods of his Lord; in fine, if he made proper use of the creatures confided to his care and dispensation, then he would receive the crown of life everlasting, in reward for his fidelity to the law and will of his Creator. But to swerve from this divine will for one moment only, thus declaring himself independent of it, as it were, would be subjecting himself to the law of God's justice, which would not fail to execute the threatened punishment.

Did God afterwards, in consideration of the most abundant efficacy of the Redemption, lay down other and easier conditions for man's happiness and salvation? He did not change His will one jot. Man's happiness was to depend on his obedience and submission to the divine will. "Now, if thou wilt hear the voice of the Lord Thy God to do and keep all His commandments, the Lord Thy God will make thee higher than all the nations that are on the earth, and all these blessings shall come upon thee, and overtake thee, yet so if thou hear His precepts." (Deut. xxviii. 1, 2.) And Jesus Christ, the restorer of grace, says: "You are My friends if you do the things that I command you." (John xv, 14.) And again: "Not every one that saith to

Me: Lord, Lord, shall enter into the kingdom of heaven, but he that doth the will of My Father, Who is in heaven, shall enter into the kingdom of heaven." (Matt. vii., 21.) He Himself gave the example, having been obedient even unto the death of the cross, thereby teaching all men that their salvation depends on their persevering obedience to the will of their heavenly Father, Who sent the Redeemer, not only to ransom their souls, but also to show them the true road to heaven, by revealing to them the will of His Father. Jesus Christ, the Redeemer, appointed the Apostles, and especially Peter, to succeed Him in His office of teaching God's will. Where Peter and the other Apostles are found in their lawful successors, there only is this true and entire will of God taught, and those only who embrace and follow it faithfully, have well-founded hopes of salvation. They who follow any other rule to obtain salvation, deceive themselves. Instead of God's will, they do their own, or follow the suggestions of the devil or those of evil-minded, perverse teachers, who substitute their own will, their own meditations, thoughts, opinions, and judgment for the will of God. They imitate Adam and Eve, who believed the devil's suggestions, rather than the infallible word of God.

This great truth, that man must do God's will in order to be saved, should ever be remembered by all those who wish to walk sincerely before God, and to save their souls. But the mere knowledge and remembrance of it will not contribute to their salvation any more than this same knowledge and remembrance did to the salvation of our first parents.

Besides this truth, another, no less important, must be borne in mind, namely:

Always to be mindful of God's will; always to honor, appreciate and love it above all things; always to understand that to embrace and follow it most punctually, cheerfully and promptly, is to embrace inseparably eternal happiness and the very Source of Life; always to see clearly that whatever is contrary to it can never be good or meritorious, nay, must be death to the soul, to return to it after having left it,—to cling to it when in possession of it, is, in itself, by no means the work of human strength, but is absolutely the effect of divine grace; for, if faith teaches us that God made all things very good, it also teaches us that they cannot remain so of themselves without God's assistance, as otherwise they would cease to be dependent on Him, which is just as impossible for us to imagine as it is to believe a logical conclusion could be right without right premises, or that a river could flow perpetually without a never-failing source. It is the Lord Who must preserve them in their good condition, especially rational creatures, men, because, by their own free will, they have it in their power to swerve from God's will and law.

For this reason Jesus Christ said: "Without Me you can do nothing"—on which words St. Augustine remarks that Jesus Christ did not say: "Without Me you cannot accomplish anything," but He said: "You cannot do anything." He means to say that without His grace we are not even able to commence any good work. "If this light of faith," said our Lord to St. Catherine of Sienna, "shineth to thee, thou wilt understand that I, thy God, know better how to promote thy welfare, and have a greater desire to do so than thou thyself, and that thou, without My grace, neither wouldst nor couldst promote it." This very thing is taught by St. Paul. In his second Epistle to the Corinthians, he writes thus: "Not that we are sufficient to think anything of ourselves, as of ourselves, but our sufficiency is from God." (Chap. iii. 5.) The Apostle means to say that, of ourselves, we are not even able to think of any good and meritorious thing. Now, if we are not able to think of anything good, how much less able are we to wish for anything good. "It is God," he writes in his Epistle to the Philippians, "Who worketh in you both to will and to accomplish according to His good will." (Chap. ii. 13.) The same thing had long before been declared by God through the mouth of the Prophet Ezechiel: "I will cause you to walk in My commandments and keep My judgments and do them." (Chap. xxxvi. 27.) Consequently, according to the teachings of St. Leo I., man works only so much good as God, by His grace, grants him to work. Hence it is an article of our holy faith, condemning the erroneous doctrine of Pelagius, that no one can do the least good work, with merit for heaven, without God's particular grace and assistance. All this being true, shall we believe that the fall of our first parents, and the sins of all their descendants, cannot be imputed to them, saying that, as God did not keep them good, by making them honor, love, and follow His will and law, they could not help losing His grace and so many natural and supernatural gifts? To maintain this would, undoubtedly, be the height of blasphemy. Hence we must necessarily come to the following conclusion : It is certain, first, that man is good in the sight of God, and has well-founded hopes of salvation only in proportion as he lives up to the will of God ; secondly, that man cannot, by his own power, keep his will good, so as always to follow God's will under all circumstances ; God, therefore, must have given him an infallible means, by the use of which he can preserve his innocence, or by the neglect of which he will become guilty before God.

The use of this means must be considered as a third great and essential truth in the way of salvation. Now, common sense tells every person to call for the assistance of another where his own means are insufficient to preserve or obtain a necessary thing. Adam and Eve knew this truth very well, but, neglecting to call for God's assistance, especially when put to trial, they lacked the efficacious grace necessary to render their will firm in keeping the commandments of God and thus preserve all their temporal and spiritual happiness. Hence their fall was their own fault. We may, then, fairly conclude that the whole mystery of man's salvation and sanctification depends entirely on his constant and proper use of this means of prayer. "As God in the natural order," says St. Alphonsus, "ordained that man should be born naked and in want of many things necessary for life, and as, at the same time, He has given him hands and understanding to clothe himself and provide for his other necessities, so, in the supernatural order, man is born unable to remain good and obtain salvation by his own strength; but God, in His infinite goodness, granting to every one the grace of prayer, wishes him to make constant use of this grace in order thereby to obtain all other graces which he needs to be enabled to keep the commandments of the Lord and be saved." Prayer is, indeed, a universal and infallible means for man to keep up his relation between his Creator and himself. Now, this is, first, a relation of continual dependence on God's goodness. By praying, man professes his belief in this dependence. As the subjects of a king acknowledge their dependence on their sovereign by paying the taxes he lays upon them, so, by offering up to the Almighty the tribute of his prayer, man acknowledges himself to be a constant mendicant before his Creator, always depending on God's goodness for food, protection and preservation, both temporal and spiritual.

Secondly. It is a relation of faith. Man does not see his Lord and God; yet he must not, on that account, less firmly believe in Him. By praying he professes his faith in an omnipotent, most wise, most bountiful God, believing that the Lord knows and is able to grant what is asked of Him.

Thirdly. It is a relation of hope. Man should hope that God will give him all the necessaries of life here below, and life everlasting in the world to come. By praying to the Lord, he professes his hope in a most benevolent God, trusting that he will really receive from Him everything necessary in time and in eternity. What often troubles and disquiets so many souls, is the uncertainty of their salvation; but, according to the Apostle, our hope for salvation ought to be immovable, firm, and secure. It will be so, undoubtedly, if it rest upon two certain foundations, one on the part of God and the other on the part of man. The certain foundation, or the certain motives on the part of God, on which our hope of salvation rests, are the power, the mercy and the truth of God, and of these the strongest and most certain motive is God's infallible faithfulness to His promise which He has made to us through the merits of Jesus Christ, to save us and give us the graces necessary for our salvation. This promise, I say, is the strongest of all the motives of our hope of salvation, because, though we might believe God to be infinite in power and mercy, nevtheless, as Juvenino well observes, we could not feel confident of God saving us unless He had given us the certain promise of doing so. But this infallible promise of God will not be fulfilled unless we pray to Him for our salvation. Hence, the foundation of our hope for salvation will be certain on our part also if we pray to God for His grace and for faithful cooperation with it. As our hope of salvation rests upon an immovable, firm and secure foundation on the part of God, and God giving every one the grace to pray, no one can reasonably fear to be lost if he really perseveres in prayer for his salvation. With St. Alphonsus he may say in truth: " I never feel more confident of my salvation than when praying." This is easy to understand. My confidence to obtain from my friend what he has promised to me, will be so much the greater the better I know his power, goodness and fidelity in keeping his promises. Now, the oftener I speak to my friend, the better will I become acquainted with his virtues. Prayer being a conversation with God, my confidence in Him will increase so much the more, the oftener I speak to Him in prayer, in which He will deign to make Himself known to me, as He has promised in the gospel of St. John, chap. xiv., 21. Thus prayer is truly the mother and nurse of hope.

Fourthly. It is a relation of charity. By prayer, man keeps up and increases this golden virtue, which is the queen of all virtues. Prayer brings the soul near to God. It is like the magnetic fluid which passes over the telegraph wire from one operator to another. By its means they communicate to each other different affairs in the same instant, on account of the swiftness with which the fluid passes. They may thus be considered to be close together, although they are really very distant from each other. Prayer brings man closer to God than the magnetic fluid does two telegraph operators, the swiftness of the former being far greater than that of the latter. Through this conductor of prayer man sends to God all his messages for his temporal and spiritual necessities, and, in a moment, all the gifts and treasures of grace are sent, in return, to the soul of man, the likeness and image of the great and perfect Original. Who can doubt that, by this close intercourse of the soul with God, the fire of divine love will be enkindled and increased in a most wonderful manner?

Fifthly. The relation between God and man is that of a father to his son. Now, God, as Father, feels an unspeakable desire to communicate His benefits to man. "My delight is to be with the children of men." (Eccles.) By the constant use of prayer, man is to furnish God with frequent opportunities to make known to him His ineffable sweetness and communicate to him the gifts of His inexhaustible treasures, requiring for them no more than the price of his prayer, notwithstanding their infinite value.

This infinite desire of God to bestow upon His image and likeness, the riches of His Divinity, will manifest itself to excess in heaven. The Lord created man to be the head, king, and crown of nature; but He Himself wishes to be man's crown in heaven. "And I shall be thy exceedingly great reward," He said to Abraham. On the part of man, this crown should be merit for having done freely and faithfully God's will on earth; on the part of God it should be grace, and therefore all the honor and glory thereof should redound to Him. By prayer this two-fold end is obtained also; for by it man obtains and preserves the good will always to live up to God's holy will. But prayer being a gratuitous gift of the Lord, all its effects must be so likewise, effects partaking of the nature of their cause. Hence, according to St. Augustine, the Lord rewarding man in heaven for his free submission to the divine will on earth, by bestowing Himself upon man, the Original upon Its likeness, does nothing else than crown Himself as it were, man's creation, meritorious life, and happy death, being altogether the gratuitous gift and effect of His unbounded love for His image and likeness. Thus it is true what St. Paul says: "What hast thou, that thou hast not received? And if thou hast received, why dost thou glory, as if thou hadst not received?" (I Cor. iv., 7.) "For of Him, and by Him and in Him are all things: to Him be glory forever. Amen." (Rom. xi., 36.) Oh, great and admirable wisdom of God, which has established for man's salvation and sanctification so easy and so infallible a means as that of prayer! What can be more important and more essential for man than the faithful fulfilment of this duty of praying? And yet, strange and painful to say, what is less understood, less anxiously attended to than this duty? The neglect, forgetfulness, or ill performance of this duty has ever been the true source of all moral evils, even of infidelity and idolatry themselves. The more man neglects to communicate with God, the true life of his soul, the more he will experience the weakness of his will to resist sin and vice; his passions, the temptations of the devil and the allurements of the world will draw him headlong from one abyss of religious errors and moral evils into another. When in imminent danger of death or of a considerable loss of fortune, as, for instance, by shipwreck or fire, or the like, the greater part of men will, indeed, remember their duty of praying to God, as the only one who can save them from death. In such dangers even infidels will take off the mask of their infidelity and make a profession of faith in an Omnipotent God, crying out: "Lord save us! We are perishing! Lord, have mercy on us,—spare our lives,—save us from this fatal accident!" This case excepted, the most of men do not care for prayer. Would to God they loved their souls as much as their bodies and the perishable goods of this world! Would to God they understood the danger in which they are of being damned to the everlasting pains of hell! Certainly, they would just as naturally feel impelled to pray to the Almighty for the grace of their conversion and final salvation.

But, alas! they love the darkness of their evil ways more than the necessary practice of the precept of prayer. Hence, as the Lord in the Old Testament found it necessary to give to His people the precepts of the Decalogue, not indeed as new laws, but rather as a renewal and development of the law of nature, the divine light of which was obscured and almost extinguished, by the crimes and perversity of man, so in like manner, the same Lord of all goodness, Who never delights in the spiritual death of man, but wishes, like a celebrated artist, to see, by means of prayer, the natural freshness of life preserved in His own image and likeness, in the soul of man, the master-piece of creation, the Lord, I say, has never failed to call man's attention to the importance and necessity of this practical truth. He has declared it in most distinct language on almost every page of Holy Scripture. "Seek ye the Lord," He says by the Royal Prophet, "and be strenghened: seek His face evermore." (Ps. civ., 4.) "Let nothing keep thee from praying always." (Eccles. xviii., 22.) What God inculcated so clearly in the old law, is still more clearly and more forcibly inculcated by Jesus Christ in the new law. "And He spoke a parable to them that they ought always to pray and not to faint." (Luke xviii., 1.) And again: "Watch ye and pray." (Matt. xxvii., 41.) This precept, always to pray and not faint, was taught and emphatically inculcated in His name by the Apostles also. "But we will give ourselves continually to prayer," says St. Peter. (Acts vi., 4.) "By all prayer and supplication," writes St. Paul to the Ephesians, "praying at all times in spirit and in the same watching with all instance and supplication for all saints." (Ephes. vi., 18.) And again: "Be instant in prayer, watching in it in thanksgiving." And to the Thessalonians he writes: "Pray without ceasing." (I Thessal. v., 17.) And to His beloved disciple Timothy: "I will, therefore, that men pray in every place, lifting up pure hands without anger and contention." (I Timothy ii., 8.) Can the necessity of prayer be more clearly and more forcibly expressed than it is in these passages of Holy Scripture? It is not said in any of them that it is well to pray, or that you may pray, you are at liberty to do so, and the like. No; in most distinct language it is said: 'You must pray,' 'pray.' Neither is it said 'you must pray now and then.' No, but 'you must pray always,' 'without ceasing;' you must 'not faint' in prayer, you must watch in it 'at all times' and 'in all places.' All these expressions imply, according to St. Alphonsus and other theologians of the Church, a formal precept of God to pray, so much so, that, in their opinion, a man who would not pray for a month, could not be excused from mortal sin.

Had we then no other evidence for believing in the necessity of prayer than the fact that Jesus Christ and His Apostles have always inculcated and insisted upon it with so much force, this fact alone ought to be sufficient to convince us of its necessity and make us profess our practical belief in it by continual application to this holy exercise. For, as we firmly believe that there are three persons in God, without requiring any other evidence for this belief than the certainty of the fact that Jesus Christ Himself taught this truth, so in like manner ought we to be firmly convinced of the necessity of prayer for the simple reason that Jesus Christ Himself taught it in most express and clear language, because being God and truth itself, He could never have taught anything to be necessary unless it were really so.

But as there is no more persuasive way of instruction than by example, our Lord Jesus Christ adopted this mode of teaching us the necessity of prayer, even before He taught it by His word. Is it not truly strange and surprising to behold the Son of God, Eternal Wisdom Itself, Who came into this world to teach men the way of salvation, to instruct them in the truths of eternal life; Who, in His childhood, might have preached and wrought miracles for the conversion of sinners just as easily as in His advanced age of thirty years; is it not very surprising, I say, to see Him spend thirty years in retirement and obscurity, unknown to the world, and losing, according to our manner of judging, His precious time and life which it would seem He would have spent more profitably in teaching men and converting them from their evil ways? But, if a wise man does nothing without a wise intention, how wise, then, must have been the intention of Jesus Christ, Supreme Wisdom Itself, in spending thirty years of His life in retirement and solitude, and three years only in teaching publicly! Truly, whosoever does not feel struck by this fact in our Saviour's life must never have seriously reflected upon it, or must feel quite indifferent towards whatever He has done for us during His mortal career. Now, what was His principal occupation during the space of thirty years? It was prayer—continual prayer. No one, however, will believe and say that Jesus Christ stood in need of it. But it was necessary that we should learn the necessity of prayer for our salvation, and be convinced of it more by His example than by His words. Thirty years of His life were consecrated to this holy exercise, and three years only to the instruction of the people, and even of this short period of three years He spent the greater part in prayer. How often did He not say to His disciples: "Withdraw a little from the multitude?" And for what purpose? In order to be more at liberty to pray. Moreover, do we not read in the Gospel that, after having spent the day in instructing the people, He would retire to a lonesome mountain, there to spend the whole night in prayer? "And it came to pass that He went out into a mountain to pray, and He passed the whole night in prayer of God." (Luke vi. 12.) This was a custom of our Saviour, as we may gather from the fact that Judas, the traitor, did not go with the soldiers to seek Him in the city of Jerusalem, but went straight on to the Mount of Olives, because He knew that Jesus was accustomed to go to that place to pray during the night.

Again, wishing to be glorified by His Heavenly Father, He prayed for it. "And lifting up His eyes to heaven, He said: "Father, the hour is come, glorify Thy Son." (John xi. 1.) On this prayer Father Crasset, S. J., comments thus: "Jesus prays His Father to glorify His body. Was it not His due? Had He not merited it? Could His Father refuse Him? Why did He ask it? God did not design to grant any favor to man, not even to His Divine Son, except by means of prayer, which is the channel through which all graces flow. 'Ask, My Son,' saith He, 'all the nations of the earth, and I will give them to Thee for Thy inheritance.' Jesus merited the empire of the whole universe, notwithstanding which He obtained it only after asking it." And how did He close His life on earth? Was it not by most touching prayer? "Father, into Thy hands I commend My spirit." (Luke xxiii. 46.) Thus His life, from the begining to the end, was but a continual practice of prayer. His glorious life is not less so. He still continues to pray for us in heaven, according to St. Paul: "Who also intercedes for us with His Heavenly Father." He has been doing this for more than eighteen hundred years, and He will continue to do so to the end of the world. He likewise intercedes for us in the Sacrifice of the Mass; for Mass is, according to the doctrine of the Catholic Church, a sacrifice of impetration, in which Jesus Christ asks of His Heavenly Father everything necessary for our temporal and spiritual welfare. Now, if we consider that Mass is said at every hour of the day, it follows that Jesus Christ, for more than eighteen hundred years, has been praying for us under the Sacramental Species, and that He will continue to do so at every hour until the end of the world. Truly, if this example of our Saviour does not open the eyes of our understanding and convince us of the necessity of prayer, it will be in vain to look for other and more striking proofs in support and confirmation of this truth. Hence St. Augustine remarks: (De Orat. Dominica) "If Jesus Christ, the Lord of heaven and earth, happy in and by Himself, and standing in no need of anything whatsoever, prays, shall man, misery itself, not pray? Jesus Christ, our Divine Physician, lies prostrate in prayer, and man, sick in body and soul, should not humble himself to pray? Jesus Christ, innocence itself, prays, and man, laden with sin, should not pray? Jesus Christ, the judge of the living and the dead, prays, and guilty man should not pray?

St. Augustine means to say that Jesus Christ came into this world to instruct us both by His words and example: "I have given you an example, that as I have done, so do you also." (John xiii. 15.) And to leave this example of His unnoticed, as it were, is to have lost common sense, to forsake the order of God's goodness in order to enter into that of His justice; to leave Him as a friend in order to have Him for an enemy; to give up the ways of His consolation in order to enter into those of His severity; to fly from His beneficent will in order to fall under the effects of His powerful will. Not to follow our Lord's example in prayer is to make all our steps wandering, our paths perilous, our plans illusions, our works useless, our pleasures miseries, our prosperity chastisement, our adversity and afflictions despair, our existence a hell wherein we shall only know bitter tears and sighs. On the contrary, to follow this example, is to place ourselves in perpetual rest and security, to oblige the Wisdom of God to govern us, His Power to defend us, His Goodness to console us, His Grace to sanctify us, His Mercy to encompass us, His Sanctity to purify us, His Happiness to defend us from evil and sustain us in good, and to make all succeed and go well with us, according to our wishes for time and eternity.

CHAPTER II.

ON THE NECESSITY OF PRAYER FOR SINNERS.

AFTER having shown so much at length the necessity of prayer in general, it might seem almost useless to show this necessity for sinners or the just in particular. But as this truth is of so vital importance in the way of salvation and sancti-

fication, it seems to me that it can never be too much discussed. This and the next chapter will confirm still more what I have said in the preceding one.

Jesus Christ, speaking of the just man, said: "As the branch cannot bear fruit of itself, unless it abide in the vine, so neither can you unless you abide in Me." (John xiii., 4.) If this be true of one who already enjoys God's grace and is His friend, with how much more right must it be applied to a sinner, who has forfeited the grace of God; for no one feels more forcibly the truth of the above-cited words, than a poor sinner. In his state of the privation of God's grace, he is like that poor little infant, which, after its birth, was cast by its cruel mother into the most filthy place of the house, where it helplessly died. In like manner the sinner, being buried in the mire of sin, feels himself helpless and unable to rise from this state and be reconciled with God. If without God's grace I am not at all able to preserve His friendship, how much less am I able to recover it after having lost it by sin? "If any one asserts," says the Council of Trent, "that, without a preceding inspiration and grace of the Holy Ghost, man can believe, hope, and love, or repent in such a manner as he ought, let him be anathema." Consider well the words: "Repent in such a manner as he ought." Behold, Judas, too, repented, for Holy Scripture says of him: "Then Judas, who betrayed Him, seeing that He was condemned, repenting himself, brought back the thirty pieces of silver to the chief priests and ancients, saying: I have sinned in betraying innocent blood." (Matt. xxvii. 3.) But this was no such repentance as is required for justification, proceeding as it did, from natural motives only, it led Judas to despair. "And he went and hanged himself with a halter." (Matt. xxvii. 5.) Man, it is true, can, by himself, commit sin and offend God grievously; but, to rise again from his fall, he cannot, except by God's assistance. I can pluck out my eyes, but to set them in right again is beyond my power. I can likewise deprive myself of the grace of God, but to restore it again to my soul without God's assistance, is more than I am able. I may cast myself into a deep well, but to get out of it again without any one's assistance is not possible. In like manner I may, by mortal sin, give myself up into the power of the devil, but to escape it again, without God's particular grace, is not within the reach of human nature. St. Peter remained chained in prison until an Angel came and said to him: "Arise, and the chains fell off from his hands." (Acts xii. 7.) Had St. Peter not been awakened by the Angel he would not have thought of rising, and should he have thought of it, he would not have been able to free himself from his fetters. In like manner, the soul which has once been chained by sin, will scarcely ever think seriously of converting and returning to God by repentance, and should it ever do so, all its natural efforts will not suffice to break the chains of sin, and free it from the slavery of the devil, if God's grace does not come to its aid. St. Anselm met one day with a child in the street, keeping a bird tied with a thin string at its feet, and seeking pleasure in letting it flutter about. The bird was always flying upwards, endeavoring to obtain its liberty, but the child soon pulled it down, and the poor animal would fall to the ground, at which the child would laugh and leap up for joy. St. Anselm looked at this play for a considerable time, and felt compassion for the bird. At once the string broke and the poor animal was free. The child commenced to cry and weep, but St. Anselm laughed and rejoiced. The spectators were astonished to see a great prelate pay attention to such a play of a child, and show compassion in the beginning and joy at the end of it. But Anselm said : "Did you see how the child amused itself with the bird ? Do you know what I thought of it ? Behold, it is thus, I said to myself, that the devil amuses himself with many souls. Having them once tied with a string, he plays with them as he pleases, drawing them from one sin into another." Some he ties by making them indifferent towards God and religion and their own salvation ; others, by enkindling in them too great love and affection for the goods of this world ; some again by the sin of avarice ; others by the sin of uncleanliness, theft, fraud and so forth. Many a one of these unfortunate souls, seeing its great misery, will sigh and groan : " Would to God that I were once free from this great misery, from the abominable habit of drinking, swearing, sinning against the angelic virtue, and visiting those bad companions ! What am I to do?" What happened to that bird happens to such a sinner also ; he wants to fly upwards to obtain his liberty, but in vain ; he feels he cannot succeed, the devil keeping him tied up and pulling him into the old sin of drunkenness, injustice, uncleanliness ; and the poor captured sinner remains a slave, and hence it is that many give up to despair ; cast off all hope of ever returning to a better life, to God's grace and friendship ; nay, many even turn so bad, so hardened, so obstinate as to resemble incarnate devils, so much so, that they would sin, in spite of God, should He even stand before them, with fire and sword in hand, to take revenge on them. Others are so miserable that they do not see their misery at all, or do not want to see it, or know anything of it, in order to feel no stings of conscience and conceive no desire of amendment. Others would like to amend, and feel the good will and desire for it, but they lack courage and energy ; others, on the contrary, have no desire and goodwill to reform ; others, no confidence ; others again lack courage, good-will and confidence at the same time. Oh, misery of miseries! Whence shall such men obtain light to understand their misery? Whence shall good-will, courage and confidence come to them to rid themselves of it? From God alone can they obtain it; He alone can grant it.

The heart of man, says Holy Scripture, is in the hand of God, withersoever He likes He turns it; or, in other words, He can, in a moment, enlighten the understanding of a sinner so as to enable him to comprehend the misery and danger of his state; He can move his will so powerfully that he forms an unalterable resolution to amend, and He can, at once, inspire his heart with so great a confidence in His mercy, that he firmly hopes for the forgiveness of all his sins. But under what condition does God dispel the darkness of the sinner's mind, the obstinacy of his will, and the diffidence and despair of his heart? Under the only one condition, that the sinner ask it of Him, for God does not wish for the sinner's death, but that he may be converted and live. Hence, He is at all times ready to receive him again into grace, provided he sincerely wishes for it. The Lord has declared this by the Prophet Ezechiel (chap. xxxiii.) upon solemn oath. But this very merciful God wills, I say, that the sinner, who feels himself destitute of all courage and firm will to amend his life, of strength and constancy to overcome his passions and evil habits, and to give up his bad companions, should ask of Him, with all humility, this courage, this firm, determined will, this constancy, this grace to change his life, for then God will not fail to assist him to remove all obstacles to His grace, and receive him again into His friendship.

The Lord's conduct towards sinners is almost like that of the Lacedemonians towards their children. Wishing to make sharp-shooters of them, they would not give them bread into their hands, but placing it high, said to them: "Behold! children, there is bread ; shoot it down if you want it." In like manner God seems to speak to sinners. Behold! helpless sinners, My grace and help is ready for you at any time ; aim at it, that is, pray to Me for it if you want it ; for, as many graces will fall down upon you, as you will shoot down by the darts of your prayer, and should you have no desire to pray for My grace, or should you not be earnest enough in asking it, ask of Me the grace to pray with all earnestness and fervor, and be sure this grace shall be given you ; but if you neglect to do so you will perish through your own fault. I have told you often enough, and again I repeat, "Call on Me and I will hear you ;" " ask and you shall receive." (John xvi. 23.) "Whatever you ask you shall receive." (Matt. xxi. 22.) And in order that no one might believe that this promise applied to the just only, I have added purposely : "Every one who asks shall receive." (Matt. vii. 7.) Every one, then, without exception, no matter whether he be a just man or a sinner, shall receive what He asks of Me, but ask he must. Thus God, in His infinite goodness, has promised to give everything to him who prays. Hence St. Alphonsus says that one of the greatest pains of the damned will be the thought that they could so easily have saved themselves by asking of God to give them true sorrow for their sins and a firm will to amend their lives. No one, therefore, says St. Alphonsus, will have an excuse before God by saying that his salvation was impossible on account of the difficulties and obstacles with which he met in the way of salvation. God will not listen to such an excuse; He will answer, if you had not strength and courage enough to overcome all obstacles and difficulties in the way of your salvation, why did you not ask Me to come to your assistance? It would have been My greatest pleasure to help you. If a man has fallen into a deep well and does not take hold of the rope let down to draw him up, no one will feel pity for him if he perish. Thus the sinner, too, is lost through his own fault, if he neglect to pray for his salvation. "For so many years, the Lord will say, did I wait in the hope you would at last commence to ask of Me the grace of true repentance and amendment of your sinful life. I would have given you this grace quicker than a man can pull another out of a well. I would have delivered you from your miserable state of sin just as fast as I delivered Jonas from the whale, for no sooner had he prayed to Me in the belly of the whale than I delivered him from all danger. To pray to Me, and to call on Me for assistance, and to be delivered and saved, is but one and thé same thing. Fire does not burn straw as fast as I forgive sinners when they ask forgiveness of Me." The woman of Cana had no sooner said, "Lord, help me," than she was heard and received the grace of conversion. The Samaritan woman, too, received the grace of conversion as soon as she had asked our Lord to give her of the wholesome water of which He was speaking to her. No sooner had the publican prayed in the temple: "Lord, be merciful to me a poor sinner," than he was forgiven and left the temple as a just man. No sooner had the good thief on the cross said to our Saviour: "Lord, remember me when Thou comest into Thy kingdom," than he was forgiven and received the promise of our Saviour that he would be with Him in paradise on that day.

Father Humolt, S. J., relates of a certain vicious young man who often sincerely wished to change his life and be reconciled again to God, that, on account of his deeply-rooted evil habits, he believed his conversion utterly impossible, and that whatever he might do would be of no avail to excite true sorrow and contrition in his heart. One day he left home to dissipate his sad and melancholy thoughts in company with others. On leaving the house he met at the door a poor beggar. As soon as he saw him, he remembered what our Lord Jesus Christ has said: " Whatsoever you have done to the least of your fellow-men, you have done to Me." He then went to take a loaf of bread, and throwing himself on his knees before the beggar, he gave it to him, thus praying in his heart: " My Lord Jesus Christ, I adore Thee in the person of this poor man; most gladly would I give Thee my whole heart, but I cannot, because it is too hardened; for this time, take, I beseech Thee, this loaf of bread which I am still able to give; do, even against my will, with my heart what Thou pleasest." Oh, the wonderful power of prayer! No sooner had he thus prayed than his heart felt a most bitter sorrow for all his sins, so much so that he shed a torrent of tears. He made a good confession, performed his penance, and ever afterwards received many extraordinary graces. (Hunolt's Eleventh Sermon on the Following of Christ.)

Would to God that all those saints of heaven who, for sometime, led a sinful life on earth, would stand before you in this moment, I would request you to put to them the following questions: Most beloved souls, how did it happen that, for some time you offended God and committed sins? They all, I am sure, would unanimously say, it was because we neglected to pray to God in the moment of temptation. But why did you not die in your sins? Why did God show mercy to you, forgiving all your offences against Him? They all would answer again, it was because we implored Him for mercy and forgiveness of our sins. But how did it come to pass that you did not relapse into your former sins, but persevered in leading a penitential life until death? And they all would again unanimously exclaim: Beloved brethren, know, that this good will, this strength and courage came not from ourselves, no, of ourselves we were weak like you, we were often tempted to commit the same old sins again, but as we had at once recourse to prayer, God assisted us and we were preserved from sin. But well-beloved blessed souls, one more question: Were the devils never able at all to make you commit a mortal sin after your conversion? Know, dear brethren, know, they would say, that the devils often tempted us most frightfully to that effect, suggesting all kinds of evil thoughts and works, but know and consider, that man, when he commences to pray is more powerful than all the devils united, so much so, that no evil spirit can do him the least injury; nay the devils fly away from a man who is praying, fearing the power God grants to his soul. No sooner did he grievously tempt us than we exclaimed, Jesus help us, Mary pray for us, save us, lead us not into temptation, deliver us from the evil of consenting to sin. By this means we were enabled to give up sin, to lead a penitential life, not to fall back into sin again and to die as holy penitents.

Would to God that now, also, some of the damned souls of hell would stand before you. As the saints confess and avow that their salvation and sanctification is owing to their prayer, so in like manner the damned would confess that their eternal damnation is owing to their neglect of prayer. What do you think would be the answer of the bad thief, crucified at the same time with our Saviour ? Listen ! he would say, I confess I was a very wicked sinner and a great malefactor during my mortal life, I committed many a murder and other evil deeds, for which I have deserved hell a thousand times, but my companion on the cross was not less guilty, and his sins cried just as much as mine to heaven for vengeance, and yet he ascended from his cross into heaven, whilst I from mine was hurled down into the depth of hell ; he rejoices forever and I am tormented in the everlasting fire of hell. What brought him to heaven ? What brought me to hell ? Behold, when hanging on the cross, he most sincerely prayed to his Lord and God : " Lord, remember me when Thou cometh in Thy kingdom." For this short prayer he obtained the forgiveness of his sins, and the promise to be with his Lord in paradise on that very day. I, on the contrary, did not pray at all, and thus I remained obstinate in my sins and died as a reprobate. In like manner all the damned would answer if commanded to tell the cause of their damnation. O most frightful language for obstinate sinners who do not wish to be converted from their evil ways and reconciled to God again! O most sweet and consoling language for all those who will pray to be delivered from their sins, and received as children of God.

Would to God I could stand on a high mountain, surrounded by all the sinners in the world! I would cry out at the top of my voice: Pray, pray, pray, and you will not die in your sins, you will be delivered from them and be saved. God does not require from you that you should go and sell everything and give it to the poor, or undergo most frightful penances, or be put to a rack, or be nailed to a cross, in order to be saved; such hard conditions as these He has not made for your salvation. He has made but the easiest in the world; all that He wishes is, that you should pray to Him and ask of Him with a sincere heart, what you need. He is still the same God, just as powerful, just as merciful to help, to forgive, to receive you into His grace as He was when He said to the good thief, "This day shalt thou be with Me in paradise." He is and will be to you the same powerful, the same merciful God that He was to St. Magdalene, the penitent, to St. Augustine, to St. Margaret of Cortona, to St. Mary of Egypt, and to many other souls whom He delivered from their sins, converting them from being sinners into saints ; but you must avail yourselves of His promise, " Amen, amen I say unto you, whatsoever you ask the Father in My name He shall give it to you." (John xvi. 23.) Jesus Christ has made this promise, it never failed to be fulfilled in any one who profited by it. Heaven and earth will pass away rather, but the fulfilment of this promise shall never fail. Lost is he who prays not ; saved is he who prays. Witnesses of this truth will be all the saints of heaven on the day of the last judgment ; witnesses of this truth will be all the damned in hell, and you also who read this, will on the day of judgment, bear witness to this truth, standing either on the right or on the left of the Divine Judge. You will be a witness of this truth with the elect on the right, if you pray ; on the left, with the damned, if you do not pray. Choose what you please.

CHAPTER III.

ON THE NECESSITY OF PRAYER FOR THE JUST.

IF a man knows that he has never deserved the good graces of a noble lord, that the friendship which he enjoys is a pure gift, without any merit on his part, and that the duration of its enjoyment depends solely and entirely on the will of that lord, would he not be obliged to ask of his benefactor not to withdraw it in case he wished always to enjoy it? Now, this is the case with the just in regard to the grace and friendship of God; it is a pure gift which no man can obtain by himself, and when obtained, no one can preserve it until death unless God assists him in so doing. To live in the grace of God until death is so great a grace that, according to the teachings of the holy Fathers of the Church, no one can merit it by any good works whatever. God must bestow this gift gratuitously, and He grants it, as St. Augustine teaches, to all those who daily pray for it. The Saint says we must pray for it *daily*, because even the just are daily in danger of losing it. It will be well here to consider this daily danger, as it will thoroughly convince us that the just stand in constant need of prayer. St. Paul the Apostle says: "He that striveth for the mastery is not crowned except he strive lawfully." (II Tim. ii. 5.) No one, says the Apostle, shall be crowned with life everlasting unless he fight lawfully, until death, against his enemies, the devil, the world and his own corrupt and perverse nature. This warfare between the just and their spiritual enemies, is always dangerous, on account of the weakness of man and the subtlety of his enemies. As to the devil, St. Peter says that "he goeth about as a roaring lion, seeking whom he may devour." (I Pet. v. 8.) He persuaded Adam and Eve to eat of the forbidden fruit ; he suggested to Cain to slay his brother Abel ; he prevailed upon Saul to pierce David with a lance ; he instigated the Jews to deny and crucify Christ, our Lord ; he induced Ananias and Sapphira to lie to the Holy Ghost ; he tempted Nero, Decius, Julian, Diocletian, and other heathen Emperors, to put the Christians to a most cruel death ; he inspired the authors of heresies, such as Arius, Martin Luther, and others, to deny certain articles of the one true Catholic faith. In like manner the devil, now-a-days, still tempts all men, especially the just, trying to make them lose the grace of God ; he tempts numberless souls to indifference towards God and their own salvation ; to others he represents the deceitful happiness of the goods, riches and pleasures of this world ; to others again, he suggests the notion of joining certain secret societies ; yes, even to conceal their sins in confession and to receive Holy Communion in this state of unworthiness ; or to cheat their neighbor in their dealings with him ; or to give themselves up to excess in drinking ; or to despair of the forgiveness of their sins, and their salvation—in a word, the devil leaves nothing undone in order to make the just fall and commit sin, attacking almost every one in his weak point, which is, for most persons, that strong natural inclination to the vice of impurity. In most men he knows how to excite the lust of the flesh to such a degree that, as St. Alphonsus says, they begin to forget all their good resolutions, nay, that they even make little account of the truths of their holy faith, losing almost all fear of hell and the divine judgments. It is an undoubted fact that the greater number of those who yield in this warfare with the devil, is far greater than the number of those who gain the victory over him. If this be true of the warfare with their weakest enemy, it is far more so of the warfare with their two other enemies, they being much stronger and more dangerous than all infernal spirits united. If all the just, who have lost their baptismal innocence, were to tell how they happened to lose it, they would all say much the same thing, viz : by such and such a person I was initiated in sin and evil deeds. I would still be innocent had I never seen that companion, that relative, that friend of mine. Bad example is like an unsound apple, one is sufficient to infect an entire heap; in the same manner, the bad example of one vicious person does more harm than all the devils united. Small, indeed, is the number of those who understand how to resist bad example. Besides, there is another truth to be considered here. St. Paul the Apostle says: "All that will live godly in Christ Jesus shall suffer persecution." (II Tim. iii. 12.) All those who endeavor to serve our Lord Jesus Christ faithfully, and persevere in His service, will have to suffer in some way or other from their fellow-Christians, neighbors, relatives, friends, infidels, heretics; from jealous, envious or otherwise perverse and suspicious men; from bad comrades, whose company they have given up; they will be blamed, rashly judged and condemned—now for such a word and manner of acting—then for some other; and what is the most painful is, that the just man is often obliged to suffer most from those very persons who, naturally speaking, ought to be his most devoted friends and companions—God thus permitting it as a trial of his patience and charity. If the number of those who come forth victorious from the struggle with the devil be small, much smaller, then, indeed, is the number of those who overcome their second enemy, the world. They suffer themselves to be influenced and dragged along by the bad example of others; they cannot bear detraction and calumny; to suffer a temporal loss is almost insupportable for the most of them; to forgive an injury or an insult is more than they can endure, so much so that they think of it day and night; try to avoid meeting those who have offended them, and bitterly complain of, nay, even curse them.

Now, how shall he be said to strive and fight against the world who cannot patiently suffer anything from it? St. Paul says: "Be not overcome by evil, but overcome evil with good." (Rom. xii. 21.) That is to say, by patience and meekness we should overcome everything that men may say or do against us. But just the contrary happens. The most men strive to overcome evil by evil; they curse, ill-treat, persecute, slander, mock all those who curse, ill-treat, slander, persecute, or scoff at them. Instead of loving, praying for, and doing good to such men, as Jesus Christ has commanded, they do the very contrary. Many will accuse themselves of it in confession, but few truly repent of their sins. What a hard task it often is for the confessor to induce such penitents to forgiveness, and not to harbor feelings of revenge.

Now, if we come to consider our third enemy, namely, our perverse nature, we shall not wonder at the saying of our Lord: "Many are called, but few are chosen." Had we not to fight with this third enemy, the devil and the world would not gain so much over us; but tnis third enemy plays the traitor, and generally gains the victory over the most of the just when the two others fail. This enemy is always near, nay, ever with us, and, therefore, more dangerous. Even the greater number of the just seem not to understand and believe this; hence it is they are so little on their guard against this enemy, who, on that account, but too often succeeds in betraying and delivering them up into the hands of the devil and his associates. And why is our corrupt nature our greatest enemy? Because, by nature, we are all inclined to evil from our infancy.

As it is natural for fire to burn, for water to flow, for the sun to diffuse light and heat, so it is, in like manner, quite natural for man to follow his passions and evil inclinations, and to commit sin as long as no superior power prevents him from doing so. Hence St. Paul said: "I do not that good which I will, but the evil which I hate, that I do." (Rom. vii. 15.) He means to say: I wish not to do evil, and I try to avoid it, but I experience within myself a continual inclination to do evil, although I wish to do good. I endeavor to do it, but I feel within myself a great reluctance thereto, and I must do violence to myself when I wish to act aright. Every one has experienced the same from his childhood, feeling more inclined to anger than to meekness; to disobedience than to submission;

to hatred than to love; to the evil desires of the flesh than to the practice of holy purity; to the gratification of the senses than to the mortification of them; to enjoying himself than to visiting Jesus Christ in the Blessed Sacrament or receiving Him in holy Communion; to indifference towards God and His holy religion than to fervor in His holy service; to the reading of bad than of good, edifying books; to listen to scurrilous talk than to the word of God; feeling more inclined, in fine, to vanity, vain-glory, pride and levity, than to humility, self-contempt and the spirit of mortification, and being ever ready to join a bad society rather than a pious confraternity of the Church. And these evil inclinations are so much the stronger the more and the longer they may have been gratified, so that we may say, in all truth, that man is more inclined to go to hell than to heaven; more inclined to follow the devil than to love God, his Maker and Redeemer. And why is this? It is because the first man, in Paradise, listened rather to what the devil told him than to the words of God. Hence this strong tendency to evil is but a just punishment of God for original sin. Baptism, it is true, cancels original sin, but it does not destroy this inclination to evil, which remains in man until death, and deservedly so.

Before Adam had committed sin, he knew not what indifference in the service of God, anger, hatred, cursing, blasphemy, impurity, vain ambition and the like were. In punishment of his sin, God permitted the inclination of man, to all that was good, to be changed into inclinations to evil. Man, then, having, by his own free will, forfeited the kingdom of God, having exchanged heaven for hell, God for the devil, good for evil, the state of grace for the state of sin, it is certainly but just and right that he should not only repent of his great prevarication, but should, as long as he lives, fight against his evil inclinations, and, by this life-long warfare against his enemies, declare himself for God and heaven, acknowledging his guilt and giving, in some measure, satisfaction to God for the great infidelity of his apostasy, thus rendering himself, in some degree, again worthy of his former rights and claims upon heaven. Taking, then, into serious consideration this continual warfare with three powerful enemies, the extreme weakness of man, and the sad experience of all ages, that the greater part of men do not overcome even one of their enemies, we see verified the words of our Lord Jesus Christ: " Wide is the gate and broad is the way that leadeth to destruction, and many there are who go in thereat. How narrow is the gate, and straight is the way that leadeth to life, and few there are that find it." (Matt. vii. 13-14.) Who will then be able to find this straight way—that is to say, who will be able to conquer, until death, these three enemies of our everlasting happiness? Whence shall come sufficient strength, courage and patience? Truly, with Josaphat, the king, we must exclaim: "As for us, we have not strength enough to be able to resist this multitude which cometh violently upon us. But, as we know not what to do, we can only turn our eyes to Thee, our God." (II Paralip. xx. 12.) By our own strength we shall not be able to overcome any one of our spiritual enemies, but by the strength that God grants to those who ask it, we shall overcome all. Prayer is that powerful means which God has given us to preserve ourselves in His grace and friendship. Should the temptations of the devil appear insurmountable, the bad example of men and the revolts of nature quite irresistible, the words of St. Paul will always be verified: "God is faithful, who will not suffer you to be tempted above that which you are able, but will make issue also with the temptation, that you may be able to bear it," (I Corinth. x. 13.) on condition, however, that we pray to Him for a happy issue with the temptation, "for," says St. Augustine, "God does not command anything impossible; if He commands anything, He admonishes you to do what you are able, and to ask Him for what you are not able, and then He will help you, that you may be able."

St. John Chrysostom speaks in the same manner: "As a city, fortified by strong walls, cannot easily be taken, so, in like manner, a soul, armed and fortified by prayer, cannot be prevailed upon by the devil to commit sin." If the soul likes to pray, the Saint means to say, prayer will be for it a wall, a dam, a bulwark, preventing the devil from doing it any injury; but, if it does not love prayer, the devil will soon conquer it, "for," continues the same holy doctor, "the devil is afraid of approaching a soul fortified by prayer, fearing the courage and strength granted by God to the soul in prayer, which strengthens and invigorates it more than food does the body." As long as the soul prays, so long will God be its strength and support, of which it will be bereft as soon as it gives up prayer.

Sin will be unavoidable; "for," continues St. John Chrysostom, "as the body, without the soul, is dead, so, in like manner, a soul without prayer is dead, emitting a bad odor"—that is to say, "the stench of all kinds of sins." A soul, then, wishing to remain in the grace and friendship of God, must love prayer, for, "as plants cannot remain fresh and green without moisture," says St. John Chrysostom, "so a soul stands in need of prayer to be saved. St. Augustine says the same in almost the same words: "As the body cannot live without food, so the soul cannot preserve the grace of God, its life, without prayer." The more, then, the soul is given up to prayer, the more it is nourished and strengthened; and the less it practises prayer, the weaker it feels. "Nay," says St. John Chrysostom, "if you do not pray you will be like a fish out of the water. As a fish must remain in water, not to lose its life, so a soul must persevere in prayer."

A plant, generally speaking, prospers only in its native soil. The same happens to the soul. God, by creating the soul, became its true home. Transplant it and it will not live. Prayer is the means by which the soul cannot be uprooted and carried away from this home by the temptations of the devil, the allurements of the world, and the sinful pleasures of the flesh. Prayer keeps the soul united to God, and God to the soul, and thus it lives happily. This is most emphatically expressed by St. John Chrysostom, in the following terms: "Every one who does not pray, and does not wish to keep up a continual communication with God, is dead, is destitute of life, nay, even of common sense; and he must be insane who does not understand the great honor of praying, and who is not convinced of the truth that not to pray is to bring death upon the soul, it being impossible to lead a virtuous life without the aid of prayer. For how would one be able to practise virtue without throwing himself incessantly at the feet of Him from Whom alone men derive all their strength and courage." (St. John Chryst., lib I., de orando Deum.) St. Augustine is of the same opinion. "He who does not know how to pray well," says he, "shall never know how to live well." (Homil. 43.) "Nay," says St. Francis of Assissium, "never expect anything good from a soul that is not given up to prayer." And Saint Bernard used often to repeat : "If I notice one who is not very anxious to pray, I at once think to myself, such a one will hardly attain any virtue." These Saints mean to say that, as we in vain seek for precious things from a poor man, so it is even more useless to expect to find virtues in one who is not accustomed to pray. Hence St. Charles Borromeo says in one of his pastoral letters : (Act. Eccl. Med., p. 1005,) "that of all means left by Jesus Christ for our salvation, prayer occupies the first place," or, in other words, that prayer is the principal means of salvation. Or, as Cornelius a Lapide says, Prayer is more necessary for Christians than any other spiritual weapon ; (In Ephes., vi. 18,) because, in the combat with temptations, God alone can grant the victory, for which we must implore His grace and assistance. "Nay," says the learned St. Alphonsus, in his preface to his little book on prayer, "in the ordinary course of Providence, our meditations, resolutions, and promises will all be fruitless without prayer, because we will be unfaithful to the Divine light and inspiration if we do not pray ; for, in order to be enabled to do good as we ought, to overcome temptations, to practise virtues, in a word, to keep the commandments of God in a perfect manner, we need, besides Divine light, meditations, and resolutions, the actual assistance of God also, which the Lord grants to those only who pray for it, and who pray for it unceasingly. Divine lights, pious considerations, and resolutions, make us pray when strongly tempted to transgress the commandments of God, and thus we obtain the Divine help necessary not to yield to the temptations; as, on the contrary, we should undoubtedly be lost, if we would not pray." Hence, St. Thomas Aquinas is of the belief that Adam committed sin because in his temptations he neglected to pray to God for assistance. St. Gelasius says the same of the fallen Angels. "In vain did they receive the grace of God, because, as they did not pray, they could not persevere." (Epist. 5., ad. Ep. in P.) Saint Alphonsus relates, in the preface to his book, "Triumphs of the Martyrs, No. 25," "that the head of an old Japanese was, in the defence of his faith, sawed off by slow degrees. After having endured this cruel torture for a long time, even to the point of death, he nevertheless died an apostate, because he had ceased to recommend himself to the Lord. Would to God that all might learn from this that our salvation depends on our perseverance in praying to God for aid to resist temptations, and to bear patiently the sufferings and adversities of this life." Father Paul Segneri relates that a young man called Paccus, in order to do penance for his sins, retired into a wilderness, where, after some years of penance, he was so violently assaulted by temptations that he thought it impossible to resist any longer, and often yielded to them. In his despair of salvation he thought of taking his own life, believing it would be better for him to die immediately, and go to hell then, than after having committed many more mortal sins, for which he would have to suffer so much the more in hell. One day he picked up a venomous snake, provoking it in every possible way, in order that it might inflict upon him a poisonous wound, but the good creature did not hurt him in the least. "Oh! God!" said Paccus, "so many men die who are so much afraid of death, and I, who wish so much for it, cannot die." He then heard a voice saying to him, "Poor wretch! do you imagine you could overcome temptations by yourself? Pray to God for assistance, and temptations will no longer injure you." Encouraged by this voice, he prayed most fervently, and obtained by his prayer such great courage and strength, that he lost all fear of temptations and the infernal spirits.

But why should I quote examples of this kind? Almost every one of us may serve as an example to prove the truth that to neglect prayer is to fall into sin and lose the grace of God. Let every one who has committed sin reflect whether he prayed in the moment of temptation, and he will be forced to avow that he did not. Every sin we commit is a standing proof of the truth that the grace of God cannot be preserved without incessant prayer. Hence, Saint Cyprian wrote to the Christians of Africa, who were daily becoming more lukewarm and less fervent in the service of God, committing sin after sin to such an extent that many fell away from the faith. " I have learned that you have become lukewarm and remiss in prayer, and that you are not watchful in it." Lukewarmness and neglectfulness in the service of God keep pace with lukewarmness and neglectfulness in prayer. As boiling water slowly cools when removed from the fire, and at last becomes cold, so the soul and will of man will cool in the love of God in proportion as he gives up prayer. Hence, if you notice sinful disorders in a family, or in a community, be sure that prayer is forgotten there. Even all victories gained by the just over their spiritual enemies will, on the day of judgment, be so many evident proofs of the truth in question. For this reason Cornelius a Lapide says, that Christians cannot make any better use of their leisure time than by spending it in prayer. The Saints, therefore, being so intimately convinced of this truth, loved and practised nothing so much as prayer. King David, knowing no other means besides prayer to escape the snares of the devil, would often say to the Lord : " Lord, look upon me and have mercy on me : for I am alone and poor."

(Ps. xxiv. 16.) "I cried with my whole heart—hear me, O Lord; let Thy hand be with me to save me." (Ps. 118.) And thus he prayed without ceasing, according to his own words in Ps. xxiv. 15: "My eyes are ever towards the Lord, for He shall pluck my feet out of the snare." And again in Ps. 118: "How have I loved Thy law, O Lord; it is my meditation all the day." Daniel, says St. John Chrysostom, preferred to die rather than to give up prayer. St. Philip Neri, being one day commanded to apply to prayer a little less than usual, said to one of his Fathers: "I begin to feel like an animal." Hence Blessed Leonard, of Port Maurice, used to say a Christian should not let a moment pass by without saying: "My Jesus, have mercy on me!" It was by means of prayer that the Saints overcame all temptations of the world, of the devil, and of the flesh. They suffered most patiently all their crosses, tribulations, and persecutions until death. The more acute and painful their sufferings were, the more they prayed, and the Lord came to their assistance; thus they triumphed over all their enemies. After St. Theodore had been cruelly treated in many different ways, he was at last commanded by the tyrant to stand on red hot *pot-sherds*. Finding this kind of torture almost too great to endure, he prayed to the Lord to assuage it, and the Lord at once granted him courage and fortitude to stand these torments until death. (Triumphs of the Martyrs, by St. Alphonsus.) By prayer alone is to be obtained courage, protection, fortitude, magnanimity, and endurance in sufferings and adversities. This we learn especially by the Angel who descended with the three children into the fiery furnace of Babylon. But the Angel of the Lord went down with Azarias and his companions into the furnace. (Dan. iii., 49.) But the angel of the Lord had already descended into the flames before them, otherwise they would have been burnt up immediately, but they did not see him before they had prayed in the manner related from verse 24 to verse 46. After that prayer, they saw him, how he drove the flame of the fire out of the furnace, and made the midst of the furnace like the blowing of a wind bringing dew. (Verse 49, 50.) Thus the Angel of the Lord wished to indicate, as Cornelius a Lapide remarks, that in persecutions and tribulations prayer is the only means to be saved. Those who made use of it have always been victorious; those who did not make use of it have universally given way and perished. "I have known," says St. Cyprian, "and I have shed tears over many who seemed to possess great courage of heart and fortitude of soul, and when on the point of receiving the crown of life everlasting, they fell away in the end and denied Him Whom they had professed for many years. What was the cause of it? They had turned away their eyes from Him Who alone is able to give strength to the weak. They had given up prayer, and commenced to look for aid and protection from man; they considered their own human weakness; the red hot gridirons, those points of iron, those swords, and all the other instruments of martyrdom so frightful to look at; and compared the acuteness of the pains with their strength, and hence it came that they lost the victory; for as soon as one thinks to himself 'I can suffer this but not that,' his martyrdom will never be crowned with a glorious end. He only who abandons himself entirely to the Divine will, and who looks for help from God alone, will remain firm and immovable and persevere to the end. But this can be expected only from him who is gifted with a lively faith which does not tremble, nor examine and consider how great the tyrant's cruelty, and how weak human nature is,—but how great is the power of the Almighty Who fights and conquers in His members. Nor should any one, on experiencing some great bodily or spiritual affliction, lose courage on that account. Let him trust in the Lord, Whose battles he fights. He will not permit any one "to be tempted beyond what he is able, but will grant a happy issue to all sufferings." Hence, we read that all the martyrs would constantly pray in their torments, and the more their pains increased the more they would pray, and thus they triumphed and gained the glorious palm of martyrdom. "We all," says St. Alphonsus, "ought to be firmly convinced that we are, as it were, standing over a very deep abyss of sin, and are kept there by the slender thread of Divine grace; if this thread breaks we fall into the abyss, and shall commit the most atrocious crimes. "Unless the Lord had been my helper, my soul had almost dwelt in hell." (Ps. lxliii., 17.) "Unless the Lord keep the city, he watcheth in vain that keepeth it." (Ps. cxxvi., 1.) "Unless the Lord preserves the soul from sin, all its endeavors will be in vain to avoid it." "Lord," exclaimed Philip Neri, "keep Thy hand over me this day, otherwise Thou wilt be betrayed by Philip." Now, what a St. Augustine, a St. Cyprian, a St. John Chrysostom, a St. Alphonsus, and many other Saints have said on prayer, as a most necessary means to preserve the grace of God until death, is confirmed by many of the clearest passages of Holy Scripture. "Woe to you that devise that which is unprofitable and work evil. . . because your hand is against God;" (Micheas ii., 1.) that is because you do not raise up your hands in prayer to God. Behold, how powerful prayer is with God, and how great the evils are that flow from the neglect of prayer. Those Israelites thought of nothing but of robbing and cheating. And how did it happen that they became so bad? It was, as the Holy Scripture says, because "they did no longer raise up their hands in prayer to God." Had they prayed to the Almighty, as the Holy

6*

Ghost gives to understand, they would have been mindful of God and His judgments, terrified by which they would have stopped perpetrating any more heinous crimes; as the Lord, on account of their prayer, would have prevented them with His efficacious grace, inspiring them to quit their evil ways, and to return to true repentance of their sinful lives. Again, how did it happen that those two elders went so far in their perverseness as to try to violate the most chaste Susannah? It was, as Daniel the prophet says, (chap. xiii., 9) because "they perverted their own mind, and turned away their eyes, that they might not look into heaven nor remember just judgments." And what does David, the royal prophet, say in this respect? Speaking of the impious, (Ps. xiii.,) "they are corrupt, and they are become abominable in their ways. . . . They are all gone aside, they are become unprofitable together; there is none that does good, no, not one. . . . . Destruction and unhappiness are in their ways." . . . He at last, in verse 5, adds the reason for their evil ways, saying: "They have not called upon the Lord." This was the cause of their wickedness. And St. Paul writes, in his second letter to the Corinthians: (chap. xiii., 7,) "Now we pray God that you may do no evil." Prayer, he means to say, will keep sin far from you. We read in the book of Machabees that Judas, the Machabee, by means of a small force, gained many great victories over Antiochus. How did this happen? It was for the fervent prayer which he addressed to God before each engagement. But Holy Scripture does not say this of him in his last battle, and hence the cause of his defeat. For him, then, says St. Isidore. (lib. 3, de summo bono, ch. 8,) who is overwhelmed with temptation, there is no other remedy left than prayer, to which he must have recourse as many times as he is tempted; for frequent recourse to prayer subdues all temptations to sin. "Which of the just," asks Saint John Chrysostom, (Sermo de Mose) "did ever fight valiantly without prayer? Which of them did ever conquer any one of his enemies without prayer?" Neither any of the prophets, nor any of the Apostles, nor any of the martyrs, nor any of the confessors, nor any of the holy virgins and widows, nor any of the just,—no matter how many thousands soever there may be, either in heaven or on earth. "Nay not to pray," a pious Jesuit Father used to say, "and yet remain free of sin; not to pray and yet persevere in good; not to pray and yet be saved, is to tempt God; is to ask of Him a miracle; is just as much as to think one can see without eyes, hear without ears, walk without feet." "We believe and are firmly convinced," we must say then with St. Augustine, "that no one can work out his salvation without the help of God, and that this help is granted to him only who asks for it?" Nay, every one must, with St. John Chrysostom, declare this to be utterly impossible, saying : " It seems to me it must be with every one a clear and undoubted truth that it is altogether impossible for one to lead a virtuous life without frequent recourse to prayer." (Lib. I, de orando.) Hence, I beseech you, brethren, I say with St. Bernard, "always to have recourse to prayer as to the surest weapon of defence." Let prayer be your first act in the morning, the commencement of all your actions ; let prayer accompany and finish them. Oppose prayer to the devil when he tempts you to lukewarmness, to impatience, to impurity, or to any other sin. With prayer arm yourself in your dealings with the wicked world, and in the combat with your own corrupt nature ; let prayer never leave your heart and lips ; let it be the faithful and inseparable companion on all your journeys; let prayer close your eyes after having gone to rest at night ; let prayer be your exercise of predilection. Any other loss can be made up for, but never that of prayer ; if, on account of a delicate constitution, you cannot fast, you may give alms ; have you no occasion to confess, you may obtain forgiveness of your sins by making an act of perfect contrition ; nay, even the Sacrament of Baptism may be supplied by the real desire of it, and a perfect love of God, but no other means of salvation is left for him who does not love to practise prayer. Every other occupation should then be given up rather

than that of prayer. Persevere in it, as Jesus
Christ and all the Saints did, closing your life and
breathing forth your last breath with it. "Father,
into Thy hands I commend my spirit." Thus, prayer
will conduct you to heaven, there to reign eternally
with our Lord Jesus Christ and all the just in everlasting joy and glory.

CHAPTER IV.

ON THE NECESSITY OF PRAYER FOR ECCLESIASTICAL STUDENTS.

"Lord, teach us to pray, as John also taught his disciples."
[LUKE xi. 1.

ONE of the most important duties of a pastor is
to teach the people the necessity and efficacy
of prayer, and how they are to pray and for what
they are to pray. Hence it is said, in the Catechism
of the Council of Trent, that "amongst the duties
of the pastoral office, it is one of the highest importance to the spiritual interest of the faithful to
instruct them in Christian prayer, the nature and

efficacy of which must be unknown to many, if not enforced by the pious and faithful exhortations of the pastor. To this, therefore, should the care of the pastor be directed in a special manner, that the faithful may understand how and for what they are to pray."

Oh! how unspeakable a pleasure is given to Jesus Christ, by a pastor, who often, either in public or in private, complies with this duty. Would to God that all pastors would adopt the sentiments of St. Alphonsus, and could say with him: "I would wish to do nothing else than speak and write on this great means of prayer; for, on the one hand, I see that the Holy Scriptures, including both the Old and New Testament, exhort us to pray, to ask and cry aloud if we wish for the divine grace ; and on the other hand, I must openly confess that I cannot help complaining of preachers, confessors and spiritual writers, because I see that none of them speak as much as they ought of the great means of prayer. And in the many courses of Lenten sermons which have been published, where shall we find a discourse on prayer ? Scarcely do we find a few passing words concerning this important means of grace. Hence I have written at length on this subject in so many of my little works, and whenever I preach, I always repeat these words : Pray, pray, if you wish to be saved and to become Saints. It is true that, to become Saints, we must have all virtues, mortification, humility, obedience, and principally, holy charity, and to acquire these virtues other means besides prayer are necessary, such as meditation, Holy Communion and good resolutions; but, unless we pray, all our Communions, meditations and resolutions will not make us practise either mortification, humility or obedience. We will neither love God nor resist temptations, in a word, we will do no good. Hence St. Paul, after having enumerated many virtues necessary for a Christian, tells us to " be instant in prayer," (Rom. xii. 12.) thereby giving us to understand, as St. Thomas remarks, " that to acquire all necessary virtues, we must always pray, because, without prayer, we would be deprived of the assistance of God, without which it is impossible to practise virtue." (Spouse of Christ on Prayer, No. 13.)

These sentiments and this practice of St. Alphonsus were common to all the Saints. Should you ever hear any one oppose them, rest assured that he cannot say in truth, with St. Paul: " I think that I also have the spirit of God (I Cor. vii. 40); nor must you believe that he is of the seed of those men by whom salvation was brought to Israel." (I Mach. v. 62.)

Let us, in imitation of the Saints who were filled with the spirit of God, never feel weary of repeating this sacred truth, in public and in private, for it is but too true, as St. Augustine says : " The understanding flies ahead, but resolution and action follow on slowly, or not at all." Our will is still weaker and more powerless to embrace what is right than the understanding is to comprehend. Hence people must often be told the same thing. Witness St. Paul, who says: "To write the same things to you, to me is not wearisome, but to you is necessary." (Philip iii. 1.) The Apostle did not want matter to write, for he who had been enraptured to the third heaven was able to say many new and sublime things, but he deemed it necessary often to repeat to them the same thing, judging this course to be the more profitable for them. Hence it was the opinion of St. Francis de Sales that a preacher should not take the least notice of those fastidious minds who are displeased when a preacher repeats a thing and goes over the same ground again. What! is it not necessary, in working iron, to heat it over and over again, and in painting, to touch and retouch the canvass repeatedly? How much more necessary, then, is it to repeat the same thing again and again in order to imprint eternal truths on hardened intellects and on hearts confirmed in evil? Now, what can be more necessary and more profitable than often to imprint on souls the doctrine of prayer?

But, alas! how does it happen that this most essential duty of a pastor is neglected by so many? It is principally because they themselves have never learned how necessary prayer is, and how efficacious if performed well.

A man will not speak what he knows not, nor will he give what he does not possess. To be enabled to discharge this pastoral duty properly, a priest must have learned, whilst as yet a student, to lead a holy life, and to practise faithfully meditation and prayer. For this reason it has seemed necessary to me to add a chapter on the great obligation under which ecclesiastical students are to sanctify themselves, in the course of their studies, by the practice of solid virtue, and by prayer and meditation, in order that, after their ordination, they may be the better enabled to inculcate this important truth of salvation the more forcibly on every mind and heart.

Above all, I must remark that I am far from believing that all who study for the priesthood are called to it. Alas! there are but too many who study from low and worldly motives, seeking, in the ecclesiastical state, nothing but temporal advantages. To this kind of students, I have but a few words to say. In order to save your souls, you ought to consider that it is necessary to embrace that state of life to which God has called you, for in that state only you occupy the place for which God has destined you from all eternity, and in it He will favor you with all the graces necessary to fulfil the duties of your state; out of it, it will be very difficult for you, not to say altogether impossible, to work out your salvation. This is true for every state of life, but is far more so in regard to the ecclesiastical state. Any one receiving Holy Orders, without having the signs of a true vocation from God, is guilty of mortal sin. This is the teaching of St. Alphonsus, and of many learned theologians, especially of St. Augustine, who says, when speaking of the punishment of Core, Dathan and Abiron, who wished to exercise the duties of the High Priest without being called thereto, " they have been damned in order that every one may be deterred from taking upon himself the office of a High Priest without being called to it by God. This fate will befall all those who, as Bishops, Priests or Deacons, intrude themselves into these holy dignities." (Serm. 98.) The reason for this is, first, because it is a very grievous presumption for one to dare to enter into the holy of holies without a divine vocation ; secondly, because such a one will be deprived of the proper means and graces to comply with the duties of this holy state, which duties, strictly speaking, he might be enabled to comply with, but having missed the right road, he will find every other very steep and most difficult to walk in, and he will be, as it were, like a misplaced member of the human body, which, indeed, may still perform some services, but not without great difficulty and many defects. Hence St. Ephrem considers as reprobates all those who dare become Priests without a divine vocation. "I am astounded," says he, "at the folly of those who are so bold as to perform the functions of the priesthood without having grace for it from Jesus Christ. Unhappy wretches, who do not know that by doing so, they are preparing for themselves everlasting fire." (De Sacerdot.) Most assuredly the sooner these students renounce their course of life the better it is for themselves and others.

Now, as to those students of whom Jesus Christ has said: "You have not chosen Me, but I have chosen you," (John xv. 16), let them consider well to what they are called. To be called to the priesthood is to be called to the highest dignity on earth, unsurpassed by any dignity whatsoever. Hence Innocent III. says of the Priest, that he is placed between God and men, and is, as such, less than God, but more than man. This dignity supposes, besides the divine vocation, positive holiness of life, which means that whosoever is to be invested with it must not only be free from sin and vice, but he must also be enriched with all kinds of virtues; for which reason the Church, during eleven centuries, excluded from this holy state every one who had committed, but once, a mortal sin after baptism, and if any one, after having received Holy Orders, fell into a mortal sin, he was deposed forever—for the simple reason that he who is not holy should not touch what is holy.

This severe discipline of the Church, it is true, has been abandoned; but, at all times, it was necessary that he who was guilty of grievous sins, and desired to receive Holy Orders, should previously have led a pure life for a considerable time. It would, therefore, be a mortal sin for one to receive any of the Holy Orders when still given up to a very sinful habit. "If I consider your vocation," says St. Bernard, "I am seized with horror, especially if no true penance has preceded."

Being well persuaded of this truth, many of the Saints did all in their power not to receive Holy Orders. For this end St. Ephrem feigned craziness; St. Mark cut off his thumb; St. Ammonis his ears and nose, and when the people still insisted upon his being ordained, he threatened to cut out his tongue also, upon which they desisted from their endeavors.

It is well known that St. Francis of Assisium could never be prevailed upon to become a Priest, because God revealed to him that the soul of a Priest must be as pure as the water which he showed him in a crystal vessel.

The Abbot Theodore was a Deacon only, and he would not even exercise the functions of this Order, because, whilst at prayer, he beheld a fiery column, hearing at the same time a voice, saying, "if thy heart is as fiery as this column, thou mayst exercise the functions of thy sacred Order."

Strange to say, there seems to be a natural instinct in every one that a candidate for the priesthood should be holy ; the least fault in him appears to be great, even in the eyes of the most perverse. "I have appointed you," says our Lord Jesus Christ, "that you should go, and should bring forth fruit, and your fruit should remain." (John xv. 16.) This fruit, that is to say, holiness of life, will not be brought forth unless a student seriously endeavors, in the course of his studies, to sanctify himself. Let him not imagine that sanctity will be infused into his soul by the sacrament of Holy Orders ; rest assured, that such as the student is, such also will be the Priest.

A light-minded student will be a light-minded Priest—a proud, unmortified and sensual student will make a proud, unmortified and sensual Priest.

You must study, it is true, to acquire the necessary science, without which you would be unfit for the functions of the sacred ministry. But, my dear friend, it is not learning, but purity of life that qualifies for the priesthood. For this reason an ancient author says of those who, full of sinful habits, still dare to receive Holy Orders : "They are more fit to be led to a place of execution than to the Church to receive Holy Orders." But it is not enough to be free of sin ; he must, moreover, have led a pious life, and have acquired a certain facility in the practice of virtue. Hence, should a candi-
7*

date for any of the Holy Orders be habitual in committing any grievous sin, especially that of impurity, at the time when he is to be ordained, he is, though he should otherwise be worthily disposed to receive the sacrament of penance, not fit to receive either. For, in order to receive the sacrament of penance worthily, he must also be disposed to receive that of Holy Orders worthily.

Hence, a Confessor, by absolving such a candidate, would make himself guilty of mortal sin, and should he give him good testimonials, on which a Bishop might ordain him, he will, moreover, render himself guilty of all those sins which such an unworthy candidate will still commit.

Holy Orders, then, to be received worthily, must be preceded by a virtuous life. St. Bernard could not refrain from weeping at the consideration that so many were hasty in receiving Holy Orders without minding the great holiness of life which is required for their worthy reception.

According to St. Thomas Aquinas, Priests must be possessed of greater interior holiness than even religious, on account of the holy and sublime functions of the sacred ministry, especially on account of the Holy Sacrifice of Mass. St. Augustine says : " A good religious will hardly make a good Priest," so that a Priest cannot be called good as yet, if he does not surpass in virtue a good religious.

My fears for students are not as to the acquisition

of knowledge, but that they will not acquire sufficient holiness of life before receiving Holy Orders. The Holy Church is not in want of learned Priests, but of very holy ones, for the reason that her candidates for the priesthood do not, whilst they are students, make sufficient efforts to sanctify themselves.

I have always observed that the greater portion of ecclesiastical students make great efforts to acquire sufficient knowledge for the sacred ministry, but small indeed is the number of those who earnestly try to lead a holy life. A certain natural ambition of appearing learned before others, united to the consideration of being surrounded by all descriptions of unbelievers and heretics, induces them to use every exertion to learn how to refute every error and defend the truth of our holy religion ; and so seriously do they apply themselves to their studies, that their minds become altogether absorbed in them. Especially will this be the case if they hear or read a consideration like the following: " We live in a most anti-christian age, principles are disregarded, and iniquity is held in veneration ; we see nothing but confusion in religion, in government, in the family circle. Sects spring up and swarm like locusts, destroying not only revealed religion, but rejecting even the law of Nature. Fraud, theft and robbery are practised almost as a common trade ; the press justifies rebellion, secret societies, and plots for the overthrow of established governments. The civil law, by granting divorce, has broken the family tie ; children are allowed to grow up in ignorance of true religious principles, their fathers being without religion or given up to the most detestable vices, or their mothers destitute of virtue and infected with the spirit of vanity in the highest degree, the natural consequence of which is that they are regardless of their parents. How great is the tendency to act contrary to the spirit of religion, manifesting itself both in education and in action. The number of apostates is on the increase, at least in the younger generation ; immoral books and tracts circulate freely ; daily journals, weekly magazines, the great organs of public opinion, become more unchristian every day, so much so that no one who has at heart the morality of his fellow men, especially of youth, can, with propriety, recommend them for perusal ; and yet how eagerly are they sought for and devoured, as it were, by every class of men. It is indeed lamentable that many whose duty it is to oppose themselves to the torrent of these and many other evils too tedious to enumerate, rather encourage them by their manner of living."

Such diseases of the human mind and heart, the student will think, require remedy. He will think that, to counteract and check them, will require much learning and information, and that, therefore, an exact and serious study of philosophy and theology will be an excellent means of stemming this torrent of moral evils. But here lies the stumbling block for the generality of students; they endeavor to cultivate the mind rather than the heart; to fill their memory with the principles of philosophy and the profane sciences rather than with the doctrines of Jesus Christ and His Saints; to care more for knowing their lessons well than for making a good meditation ; to trouble themselves more for appearing prepared before their professor and school mates than before Jesus Christ in Holy Communion ; they will endeavor to find the best way of connecting one point with another in a discourse, rather than making a good examination of conscience ; to be more anxious to acquire a reputation for learning and great capabilities than for true humility and sincere charity ; they will be more pleased with the flatteries and praises of the world than the good pleasure of Jesus Christ and His holy Angels ; to be able to show acuteness in reasoning, and ability in delivering a learned discourse, will be with them of greater weight than to manifest the spirit of meekness, forbearance, condescension, obedience and submission in all their words and actions. Their desire will be more for profane, frivolous books, than for those which nourish piety and inspire love for solitude and prayer. In a word, they will make greater efforts to acquire the wisdom of the world than that of Jesus Christ and His Saints. To this end all of their thoughts, words and actions will be directed, and thus study becomes for them rather a means of greater separation from God than of closer union with Him.

My complaint of students is not for their application to studies, but for their attaching too much importance to them, and for the erroneous manner by which they acquire the various sciences. I consider that many students attach too much importance to sciences, imagining that by means of them they will convert the world.

Now, learning can do something, it is true, but however much it may accomplish, experience teaches in the present as in the past, that moral evils never yield to any force but that of the grace of God. A learned man may enlighten the mind of his fellow men and expel its darkness and errors, but for all that their hearts will not embrace the truth. Hence St. Vincent de Paul, writing to one of his priests, says: "No, it is neither philosophy, nor theology, nor eloquence which moves the soul." This was felt keenly by St. Bernard whilst at Paris, 1123, where he was invited by the high schools to deliver a learned discourse on one of the principal questions in philosophy. Having prepared himself most carefully for the occasion, he delivered an eloquent discourse before a large auditory, but without making the least pious impressions on his hearers. This made him sad and ashamed of himself, so much so that, shutting himself up in his room, he lamented his failure with many sighs and tears, and with earnest prayer to God, implored the Divine assistance.

The day after he spoke again in public, but now it was the Holy Ghost that spoke by his mouth and guided his tongue, and his discourse made so deep an impression on his hearers, that several priests followed the Saint to Clairvaux, there to lead a perfect life under his wise direction. (History of St. Bernard by Theo. Ratisbonne, vol. I., chap. 11.) It is related in the life of this saint, that mothers would keep their children, wives their husbands, and friends their friends from hearing him, because the Holy Ghost gave such great power to his words that no one could resist them, but every one felt drawn to follow him or lead at least altogether another life.

Alas, there are but too many who imitate St. Bernard in his first discourse at Paris. Like him they, too, know how to prepare most learned discourses, lectures, sermons and instructions, using the most eloquent terms of the language to convey their ideas to the minds of their hearers, but they fail in reaching the heart, and derive from their efforts no other fruit than a few remarks from the people, calculated to flatter their self love and nourish pride. "How well," they will say, "he has acquitted himself! What an eloquent tongue! What profound knowledge! What an admirable memory! What a fascinating preacher! What a pleasure it is to listen to such a man! I never had such a treat in my life!" Would to God they would imitate St. Bernard in his preparation for his second discourse; how different would be the fruit of their labors. Let us hear the saints in reference to this point. "You must consider," says St. Vincent de Paul, "that learning without humility has ever done much harm to the Church, that pride has always led the most of learned men, like the rebellious angels, to everlasting perdition, and that God does not need learned men to carry out His wise designs and accomplish His works. Nay, that generally speaking, He makes use of the simple to convert men and procure the welfare of His Church, as He did of the Apostles, and in recent times of St. Catherine of Sienna, and of St. Teresa," and of late, I may add, of the Curé of Ars in France. St. Ignatius says, "it is of greater importance for students to advance in virtue than in science; if they cannot do both at the same time, virtue must have the preference, minus scientiæ, plus virtutis." (Life by C. Genelli.) St. Francis of Assisium said to those who, on entering his order, were already scientifically prepared, and wished to apply themselves to the study of Holy Scripture: "I am well pleased with this, provided, according to the example of Jesus, Who seems to have devoted more time to prayer than to anything else, they do not neglect the exercise of prayer, and study to practise what they have learned rather than to know what they have to speak." "The truths of the Gospel," he would say, "are better understood by those who practise them than by those who know them, but neglect to put them into practice. A man possesses knowledge and eloquence only in as much as he practises what he knows and says. We behold many who endeavor to acquire great learning, but happy is he who knows Jesus Christ crucified." Those studies which are applied to from the motive of vanity, to earn the praises and flatteries of men rather than from the pure motive to gain souls to God, were an abomination in his eyes. "In the day of tribulation," he would say of these men, "their hands will be empty; it would be better for them now to endeavor to be strengthened and confirmed in virtue in order to have the Lord for support at that time, for the time will come when books will be rejected as useless articles. My brethren should, therefore, endeavor to be grounded in humility, simplicity, in prayer, and in the virtue of poverty. This is the only sure way of edifying their neighbor and of procuring his salvation, because they are called to imitate Jesus Christ, Who did not follow or show any other road. Many will abandon these virtues under the specious pretext of edifying their neighbor by their learning, but they will go so far that the possession of sciences by which alone they thought they would be filled with light, devotion and love for God, will be for them the cause of interior coldness and emptiness. Hence, it will come to pass that, having lost their time in vain and false studies to live up to the spirit of their state of life, they will find themselves incapable of returning to their primitive vocation."

St. Francis was by no means averse to sciences, on the contrary, he inculcated to his brethren, whose duty it was to teach others, to apply themselves properly to study ; but he always opposed strenuously that vain, proud science, which is always without devotion, preaching itself instead of the Crucified. He would always have before his eyes the following passages of Holy Scripture : "Many will say to Me in that day, Lord, Lord, have we not prophesied in Thy Name, and cast out devils in Thy Name, and done many miracles in Thy Name? And then will I profess unto them, I never knew you ; depart from Me, you that work iniquity." (Matt. vii. 22-23.) And again : "If I speak the tongues of men and of Angels, and have not charity, I am become as a sounding brass or a tinkling cymbal." (I Corinth. xiii. 1.) And: "I chastise my body and bring it into subjection, lest, perhaps, when I have preached to others, I myself should become a cast away." (I Corinth. ix. 27.)

Besides, he was aware that man is naturally more

inclined to know than to practise, and that virtues which purify the soul are more necessary and more precious gifts than learning, which enlightens the mind only. He knew very well that "knowledge puffeth up," (I Corinth. viii. 1) and that a learned man is easily inclined to be proud and self-conceited if Christian charity does not keep him humble.

St. Alphonsus spoke in the same manner : " The Apostle St. Paul," said he, " wrote of this world's wisdom : ' Knowledge puffeth up, but charity edifieth. If any man think he knoweth anything, he hath not yet known as he ought to know.' I Cor. viii. 1-2.)

Knowledge, united to the love of God, is most useful to us and to our neighbor, but if charity does not accompany it, it does us much harm by making us proud and leading us to despise others ; for the Lord is merciful to the humble, but severe to the proud. Happy is the man to whom God has given the wisdom of the Saints, which He bestowed on the righteous Abel. ' He gave him the knowledge of the holy things.' (Wisdom x. 10.) The Holy Spirit speaks of this as the greatest of all gifts. How many do we not see who are puffed up because they understand mathematics, literature, languages and antiquities ? What does religion gain by their knowledge? What do they do for their own spiritual advancement ? What do those numerous learned men gain from their knowledge whose mind, though adorned with so many acquirements, know not even how to love God so as to practise virtue.

The Lord refuses His light to those sages of the world who only labor to obtain self-renown, and he grants them only to the simple. 'I confess to Thee, O Father, Lord of heaven and earth, because Thou hast hid these things from the wise and prudent, and hast revealed them to little ones.' (Matt. xi. 25.) By little ones are to be understood those only who seek to please God. 'Happy,' says St. Augustine, 'is he who knows God, His Greatness and His Goodness, though he be ignorant of all besides; for he who knows God cannot help loving Him. Now, he who loves is wiser than all the learned of the earth who have not this love.'

'The ignorant arise,' exclaimed the same Doctor, 'and obtain heaven! How many ignorant people, how many poor villagers sanctify themselves day by day and obtain eternal life, a single instant of which is preferable to the enjoyment of all the goods of the earth.' St. Paul wrote to the Corinthians: 'I judged not myself to know anything among you but Jesus Christ and Him crucified.' (I Cor. ii. 2.) Happy are we if we acquire the knowledge of Jesus Christ, of the love He has shown us on the cross. Verily, by studying the books of the crucifix, we shall come to love Him with love more than common.'

And on another occasion, St. Alphonsus said:

"We must study, it is true, because we are laborers, but we ought to be fully persuaded that the one thing needful, and that which Jesus Christ requires above everything else is, that we should endeavor to be saved as Saints. We must study, but the sole object of study ought to be that of pleasing God, otherwise it will only cause us to be a long time in purgatory, nay, even lead some, perhaps, into the torments of hell, which may God forbid. Let your aim, then, always be the glory of God and the good of souls, and when an opportunity occurs of seeming ignorant, do not recoil from it, for it will not hurt you."

An ecclesiastical student, then, must consider knowledge, in itself, only as a sounding brass, a tinkling cymbal, a source of pride, and of many other great evils; or as a sharp knife, which, if not handled well, may cause serious, even mortal wounds to the soul. This consideration must be for him a great incentive to study in a proper manner and spirit.

I will now place before you the wise advice which we find in the writings of learned and saintly men, on the holy manner and right spirit of studying.

We read of Blessed Balthasar Alvarez, S. J., that he employed all possible care to prevent studies from doing harm to piety. He succeeded in doing so by the following means:

First. Above all, he tried to inculcate to the stu-

dents' minds some striking truths, such as these—
virtue and knowledge are the two trees planted by
God in Paradise ; they are the two luminaries, the
one greater, the other smaller, created by Him to
light up the world ; they are the two Testaments,
the Old and the New Law, and Grace ; they are
the two sisters, Martha and Mary, living under one
roof in great union and harmony, and giving support to one another. Holiness gives authority and
weight to knowledge. Knowledge, if only theoretical, is indeed very poor to persuade ; it is the
living up to it that gives it persuasive power.
Hence the Apostle said to Timothy : "Take heed
to thyself and to doctrine ; for, in doing this, thou
shalt both save thyself and them that hear thee."
(Tim. iv. 16.) From this truth he derived another
one on which he insisted very much, viz : that the
acquisition of knowledge becomes so much the easier
the more one endeavors to acquire virtue. " Who
does not know," said he, " that knowledge is a gift
of God, Who communicates it so much the more
readily to those who ask it the more they purify
their conscience." Hence, an ecclesiastical student
should make greater efforts to avoid sin and correct
his faults than to study learned authors, and run
through many books. For, according to Cassian,
"it is purity of life that enlightens the mind and
sees God." To such a one it is given to understand
everything without difficulty.

Secondly. This zealous director of souls was not less careful to inspire the students with love for mortification as another means to make them advance equally in perfection and science.

But who would imagine that mortification could be an aid for advancing in science? Nevertheless, he knew how to persuade them of this also. "Try it," he said, "especially in regard to study, and you will find out that there is nothing better calculated to remove difficulties. For by mortification you will overcome your enemy, and your natural desire tempting you to occupy your mind with study when there is no time for it, as, for instance, at the time of prayer. By it, you will do violence to pride, which feels hurt by the questions of the Professor, and the objections of your fellow-students."

Thirdly. Mortification will induce you to apply only to such branches of science as are assigned for you, and to learn only what is useful, and not what is an incentive to curiosity.

Fourthly. By it you will prefer the advice of your professors to your own views and opinions, studying one thing and not another. This was the counsel of St. Augustine when he said, "That student knows much who knows how to profit by the advice of his professor. If the latter has the eyes of knowledge, the former should have the eyes of docility." "You ought to look upon yourselves as so many little children," said St. Alphonsus. "It is for the master to judge what is fit for you, and to supply you with the occupations which may be best fitted to cultivate your minds. Many remain ignorant for wishing to know too much."

Fifthly. By it you will be prevented from boasting before others of more knowledge than you really possess, and from pretending to acquirements which you have not.

Sixthly. Mortification will make you study diligently and perseveringly, for by it you will overcome a certain disgust and reluctance, a certain laziness and indolence, trying to keep in your room and avoid useless conversation.

Seventhly. By it you will study without anxiety of heart and mind. Nothing is more detrimental to the acquisition of solid science than overgreat anxiety in studying, in consequence of which everything is superficially learned. As discretion is a virtue, so too much ardor is a vice. "Sapere, et sapere, ad sobrietatem."

Eighthly. By mortification you will overcome both a certain shame to ask for an explanation of such things as you do not fully understand, and a certain laziness to take a memorandum of what was explained, or of useful things which you read. "Multa scribendo didici," says St. Augustine.

Ninthly. From a spirit of mortification you will refrain from looking through the Sacred Orators during the course of study, and from making a selection of subjects for the pulpit. "This is but a mere temptation," said St. Alphonsus, "because by that you neglect what is essential for a mere accessory." To collect materials with any good result, he ought to have finished his studies, for otherwise he derives no profit from it, and does not study as he ought.

He often impressed on the minds of the students the necessity of studying with a pure intention. "The life of a student," he would say, "is, in itself, a very quiet one, and how little soever his efforts may be to regulate it well, he will easily learn a good deal without relaxing in zeal and fervor for his perfection. Should his fervor diminish, it will certainly be his own fault, which, no doubt, he will avoid, if he always endeavors to study with a pure intention. "The right manner of learning," says St. Bernard, "is to know the true end for which everything should be learned, namely, not to study to obtain food for vain glory, and for the spirit of curiosity, or for something similar, but for one's own edification, or for that of our neighbor. There are some who wish to know merely for the sake of knowing. This is a detestable curiosity; others wish to know in order to become known themselves, and this is an execrable vanity; others again, learn in order to sell their science, and this is hateful profit. But there are others who try to acquire learning in order to be enabled to edify their fellow men, and this is Charity. Others, again, apply to the study of sciences in order to edify themselves, and this is Wisdom. These two latter kinds of men do not abuse knowledge, studying as they do, in order to do good." (Serm. 26 in Cantel.)

A student, then, to comply in peace of heart with his duty of advancing in piety and knowledge at the same time, must have in view no other object than the good pleasure of God. It is something great, Father Alvarez used to say, to know theology, but what greater fruits can he derive from it than to learn by it so to regulate his life as never to wish for anything contrary to God's holy will. Hence, he will not feel uneasy if he does not learn more than he can or is allowed. "Let us not feel disturbed about not knowing what God does not wish us to know. To know that He does not will it must suffice to resign ourselves to His adorable will." "Knowledge," says St. Bonaventure, "which is neglected for the sake of virtue, will afterwards be acquired easily by virtue."

Finally, he spared no efforts and trouble to inspire the students with a great love for prayer, as a most efficacious means to make rapid progress, both in virtue and in science. He knew this but too well by his own experience, but his modesty would not allow him to speak of himself, hence he would cite to them the example of the Abbot Theodore, of whom Cassian relates that he had acquired great learning, more by endeavoring to purify his heart, and by assiduous application to prayer, than by reading many books. On a certain day, wishing to know the meaning of a passage of Holy Scripture, he studied long over it without success. He commenced to pray, and at once he understood its meaning."

It was by prayer that Solomon obtained his great wisdom, and taught us to obtain it by the same means. "Give me Wisdom that sitteth by Thy throne, and cast me not off from among Thy children; for I am Thy servant, a weak man, and of short time, and failing, short of the understanding of judgment and laws. Send her out of Thy holy heaven, and from the throne of Thy Majesty, that she may be with me, that I may know what is acceptable to Thee. For she knoweth and understandeth all things. The thoughts of men are fearful, and our counsels uncertain. For the corruptible body is a load upon the soul, and the earthly habitation presseth down the mind that museth upon many things, and hardly do we guess aright at things that are upon earth, and with labor do we find the things that are before us. But the things that are in heaven, who shall search out; and who shall know Thy thoughts, except Thou give wisdom, and send Thy Holy Spirit from above. And so the ways of them that are upon earth may be corrected, and men may learn the things that please Thee. For by wisdom they were healed, whosoever have pleased Thee, O Lord, from the beginning." (Wisdom 9.)

And in the next chapter, he praises the wonderful deeds which, by means of this wisdom, were performed by Adam, Lot, Jacob, Joseph, Moses, and the Hebrews. "This wisdom," says Solomon, "preserved him that was first formed by God, the father of the world, (Adam) when he was created alone, and she brought him out of his sin, and gave him power to govern all things."

She delivered the just man (Lot) who fled from the wicked that were perishing when the fire came down upon Pentapolis. She conducted the just when he fled from his brother's wrath (Jacob flying from Esau) through the right ways, and showed him the kingdom of God, and gave him the knowledge of the holy things, made him honorable in his labors, and accomplished his labors, that he might overcome and know that wisdom is mightier than all.

She forsook not the just when he was sold, (Joseph) but delivered him from sinners. She went down with him into the pit, and in bands she left him not, till she brought him the sceptre of the kingdom, and power against those that oppressed him, and showed them to be liars that had accused him, and gave him everlasting glory.

The delivered the just people (Israelites) and

blameless seed from the nations (Egyptians) that oppressed them. She entered into the soul of the servant of God, (Moses) and stood against dreadful things, in wonders and signs."

In the same manner St. Anthony, the Hermit, asked wisdom of God, and obtained it.

"He was," says St. Athanasius in his life, "very wise, and what was most admirable in him was, that he was most ingenius, most discreet, constant, and meek, although he had never studied anything. Heathen philosophers came to him, believing they would be able to deceive him by their arguments. But he answered them, 'If you have come to a fool then your trouble is useless, but if you consider me as a wise man, then imitate what you see. Had I come to you, I would try to imitate you; but as you have come to me as to a wise man, you should be what I am—Christians.' The philosophers admired the acuteness of his mind.

St. Anthony asked them again: 'Which of these two is the best, good sense or knowledge, and what is the beginning of either? Does good sense proceed from knowledge, or knowledge from good sense?'

When they answered him, that good sense was the author and inventor of science, he said, 'Well, then, he who has perfect good sense needs no science.' Just as if he said, 'I am one who never applied to acquire knowledge, but I am taught by God.'"

St. Ambrose, too, obtained wisdom in the same manner, as Paulinus relates in his life: "When he dictated the forty-third Psalm, I saw come upon him a little flame of fire, (indicating the Holy Ghost) which sat down upon his head, and by degrees entered his mouth, as into a house there to live, after which his face became like snow."

When the Abbot Rupert was required to tell who were his fathers and teachers, he answered, "I hereby confess that to be visited from above is better for me than ten fathers and teachers. I dictate whatever that heavenly monitor suggests to me."

St. Thomas Aquinas publicly avowed that he owed his wisdom more to prayer than to his efforts in studying.

When St. Ephrem prayed, saying, " Pour out, O Lord, upon me the waters of Thy grace," he received in a vision from the angels, a book, and with it heavenly wisdom, and the gift of eloquence to such a degree that howsoever overflowing the source of his words was, they never could fully express what he had conceived in his mind. For the profoundness of his doctrine and the quickness of his thoughts were such as to absorb his tongue, so that it was unable to speak out the conceptions of his mind. (Life by Nyssenus.)

In our own times we have a most striking example in the Curé of Ars. "How could this man," says the writer of the "Spirit of the Curé of Ars," "who had nearly been refused admittance into the great seminary because of his ignorance, and who had, since his promotion to the Priesthood, been solely employed in prayer, and in the labors of the confessional, how could he have attained to the power of teaching doctrine, like one of the Fathers of the Church? Whence did he derive his astonishing knowledge of God, of nature, and of the history of the soul? How was it that his thoughts and expressions so often coincided with those of the greatest Christian geniuses, St. Augustine, St. Bernard, St. Thomas Aquinas, St. Catherine of Sienna, St. Teresa?"

The spirit of God has been pleased to engrave on the heart of this holy Priest all that he was to know, and to teach to others. And it was the more deeply engraved as that heart was the more pure; the more detached and empty of the vain science of men; like a clear and polished block of marble ready for the chisel of the sculptor.

The faith of the Curé of Ars was his whole science; his book was our Lord Jesus Christ. He sought for wisdom nowhere but in Jesus Christ, in His death and in His Cross. To him no other wisdom was true, no other wisdom useful. He sought it not amid the dust of libraries, not in the school of the learned, but in prayer, or on his knees, at his Master's feet, covering his Divine feet with tears and kisses; in the presence of the Holy Tabernacle, where he passed his days and nights, before the crowd of the Pilgrims had as yet deprived him of liberty day and night, *he had learnt it all.*

Thus prayer is a most powerful means of becoming truly learned. "If any one wants wisdom let him ask it of God, who giveth to all men abundantly, and it shall be given to him." (James i., 5.)

But there are, besides this, other reasons of greater weight, and more persuasive for an ecclesiastical student to apply himself earnestly and assiduously to prayer. "In order to be enabled to draw souls to God, he himself must first be drawn by God," says St. Alphonsus. But this is done in prayer only. Men truly holy and Apostolic knew this but too well. Hence, we read in the lives of St. Dominic, St. Francis Xavier, St. Francis Regis, St. Alphonsus, Blessed Leonard of Port Maurice, that having labored during the day for the salvation of souls, they would at night retire to pray.

For this reason Father Vincent Caraffa, in writing to the young ecclesiastics, who applied to study in order to save souls, addressed to them the following remarkable words: "In order to effect great conversions, much prayer is of far greater service than eloquence. Eternal truths make quite a different impression when they proceed from the heart, than when they are preached from the lips. Hence, the practice of ministers of the Gospel ought to be in conformity to their teaching; in a word, they ought to show that they are quite detached from the world, and from themselves, and only occupied in procuring God's glory, and making Him loved by all."

St. Francis de Sales confessed of himself that his Masses and prayers had contributed more towards the conversion of the province of Chablais than all his talents. "The Apostles," said he, "never preached the word of God without having sent most fervent prayers to heaven. Deceived is he who wishes to convert infidels, heretics, or great sinners, by other means than those which Jesus Christ and his Apostles made use of. God alone can, by His grace, change the hearts of men, for which we can never sufficiently pray."

"The labor of a Priest who is not given up to prayer," says St. Vincent de Paul, "will be of little or no avail, whilst, on the contrary, with prayer, he will touch hearts and convert souls. Yes, give me a man of prayer, and all things will succeed with him. He will be able to say, with St. Paul, 'I can do all things in Him Who strengtheneth me.' Prayer is a large sermon book, by means of which they will draw the eternal truths from their source, and then communicate them to the people."

Indeed, such a one may say with our Lord Jesus Christ, "I speak that which I have seen with My Father," (John viii., 38,) and with St. John, "That which was from the beginning, which we

9*

have heard, which we have seen with our eyes, which we have looked upon, we declare unto you that you also may have fellowship with us, and our fellowship may be with the Father, and with His Son, Jesus Christ." (John i., 1, 3.) What the people said of Jesus Christ, they will say also of him. " He was teaching as one having power, and not as the Scribes and Pharisees." (Matt. vii., 29.)

"St. Francis de Sales," said the Duchess de Montpensier, in speaking of this Saint, "has done me an immense harm, since all other preachers of the word of God do no longer please me, because, whilst others are losing themselves in lofty language, he endeavors to catch souls by attacking the hearts and rendering himself perfect master of them."

" The Curé of Ars is a most admirable example of this truth. When persons have heard this saintly priest so ready to proclaim his ignorance, discourse upon heaven, on the sacred Humanity of our Lord, on His dolorous passion, His Real Presence in the Most Holy Sacrament of our altars, on the Blessed Virgin Mary, her attractions, and her greatness, or the happiness of the Saints, the purity of the Angels, the beauty of souls, the dignity of man, on all those subjects which were familiar to him, it often happened that they came away from the discourse quite convinced that the good Father saw the things of which he had spoken with such fullness of heart, with such eloquent emotion, in such passionate accents, with such abundant tears; and, indeed, his words were then impressed with a character of Divine tenderness, of sweet gentleness, and of penetrating unction, which was beyond all comparison. There was so extraordinary a majesty, so marvellous a power in his voice, in his gestures, in his looks, in his transfigured countenance, that it was impossible to listen to him and remain cold and unmoved.

"Views and thoughts, imparted by a Divine light, have quite a different bearing from those acquired by study. Doubt was dispelled from the most rebellious hearts, and the admirable clearness of faith took its place before so absolute a certainty; an exposition at once so luminous and so simple.

"The word of the Curé of Ars was the more efficacious because he preached with his whole being. His mere presence was a manifestation of the truth, and of him it might be well said that he would have moved and convinced men even by his silence. When there appeared in the pulpit that pale, thin and transparent face, when you heard that shrill, piercing voice, like a cry, giving out to the crowd sublime thoughts, clothed in simple and popular language—you fancied yourself in the presence of one of those great characters of the Bible, speaking to men in the language of the Prophets. You were already filled with respect and confidence, and disposed to listen, not for enjoyment, but for profit.

" To those to whom it was given to assist at his catechetical instructions, two things were equally remarkable—the preacher and the hearer. They were not the words that the preacher gave forth—it was more than words; it was a soul, a holy soul, all filled with Faith and Love, that poured itself out before you, of which you felt in your own soul the immediate contact, and the warmth. As for the hearer he was no longer on the earth; he was transported into those purer regions from which dogmas and mysteries descend. As the Saint spoke, new and clear views opened to the mind—heaven and earth, the present and the future life, the things of Time and Eternity, appeared in a light that you had never before perceived.

" When a man coming fresh from the world, and bringing with him worldly ideas, feelings and impressions, sat down to listen to his doctrine, it stunned and amazed him; it set the world so utterly at defiance, and all that the world believes, loves, and extols. At first he was astonished and thunderstruck, then by degrees he was touched and surprised into weeping like the rest.

"No eloquence has drawn forth more tears, or penetrated deeper into the hearts of men. His words opened a way before them like flames, and the most hardened hearts melted like wax before the fire. They were burning, radiating, triumphant; they did more than charm the mind; they subdued the whole soul, and brought it back to God. Not by the long and difficult way of argument, but by the paths of emotion, which lead shortly and directly to the desired end.

"He was the oracle that people went to consult, that they might learn to know Jesus Christ. Not only the sinful, but the learned, not only the fervent, but the indifferent, found in it a Divine unction which penetrated them, and made them long to hear it again. The more they heard, the more they wished to hear; and they always came back with love to the foot of that pulpit as to the place where they had found beauty and truth. Nothing more clearly showed that the Curé of Ars was full of the Spirit of God, who alone is greater than our heart. We may draw from His depths without ever exhausting them, and the Divine satiety which He gives only excites a greater appetite.

"The Curé of Ars spoke without any other preparation than his continual union with God. He passed without interval or delay from the confessional to the pulpit; and yet he showed an imperturbable confidence which sprang from complete and absolute forgetfulness of himself. Besides, no one was tempted to criticise him. People generally criticise those who are not indifferent to their opinion of them. Those who heard the Curé of Ars had something else to do—they had to pass judgment on themselves.

"This real power of his word supplied in him the want of talent and rhetoric. It gave a singular majesty and an irresistible authority to the most simple things that issued from those venerable lips. He loosed his words like arrows from the bow, and his whole soul seemed to fly with them.

"In these effusions, the pathetic, the profound, the sublime, was often side by side with the simple and the ordinary. They had all the freedom and irregularity, but also all the originality and power of an improvisation. We have sometimes tried to write down what we had just heard, but it was impossible to recall the things which had most moved us, and to put them into form. What is most Divine in the heart of man cannot be expressed in writing." (The Spirit of the Curé of Ars.)

Alas, how true is that saying of St. Thomas of Villanova: "Experience shows every day that a priest of moderate learning, but full of the love of Jesus Christ, converts more souls than several learned orators put together, whose eloquent discourses charm whole populations. With fine thoughts, curious allusions and ingenious reflections, it is easy to send away the auditors in admiration, but they also return cold in Divine love, and perhaps colder than they were before. Of what use are such discourses to the people and the preacher? They only serve to render him more vain and more culpable towards the Divine Majesty.

To convert sinners, and draw them out of the mire of vice, requires arrows of fire, or words full of Divine love."

Hence, St. Jerome would say that "One man inflamed with this love is sufficient to convert a whole nation."

"One word," says St. Alphonsus, "uttered by a priest inflamed with Divine love will produce more good than a hundred sermons composed by a great Divine, who has but little love for God."

"A polished discourse," says St. Jerome, "only gratifies the ears; one which is not so, makes its way to the heart."

"I have always said ever since," says St. Francis de Sales, "that whoever preaches with love, preaches sufficiently against heresy, although he may not utter a single word of controversy against it. For these thirty-three years that God has called me to the sacred office of breaking the bread of His Word to the people, I have certainly remarked that practical sermons, wherein the subject is treated with devotion and with zeal, are so many burning coals thrown into the faces of the Protestants who hear them; that they are always pleased and edified by them, and are thereby rendered more docile and reasonable when we come to confer with them on disputed points."

Now, it is not in the study of books, but in holy prayer and meditation, that the hearts become enkindled with Divine love, zeal and devotion. For this reason, St. Alponsus exclaims : " Alas ! how much more did St. Philip Neri learn in the catacombs of Rome, where he spent whole nights in prayer, than in all the books he studied ? How much more did St. Jerome learn in the grotto of Bethlehem than in all his other studies."

St. Paulinus writes (Ep. 27) : " Let the philosophers of this world have their philosophy ; the rich their riches ; kings their kingdoms, our wisdom, our riches ; our kingdom is to know Jesus Christ." Hence we must exclaim, with St. Francis of Assisi : " My God and my all !" For this reason, an ecclesiastic ought so to study as to make, at the same time, greater progress in the science of the Saints, in prayer, and in the love of God, than in the acquisition of other sciences.

" It will often happen," says St. Alphonsus, " that in prayer you will learn more in one moment than in a ten years' study."

" Incomparably greater knowledge of God," says St. Bonaventure, (Theo. Myst. c. 3, p. 2.) " is communicated to the soul by a strong desire of being united to Him in love than can be obtained by any study whatever."

" Great talents are required," says St. Alphonsus, " to acquire profane sciences, but to acquire the science of the saints, one needs but a good will."

" He who loves God more," says St. Gregory,

" has also a greater knowledge of Him." He who relishes God by loving Him sees and knows Him more clearly. He who has tasted of honey knows more of it than all the philosophers who explain its nature without having ever tasted it.

Moreover it takes much time and trouble to acquire profane sciences, but to acquire the science of the saints it suffices, says St. Alphonsus, " to will it earnestly and ask it of God." The wise man says, " wisdom is easily seen by them that love her, and is found by them that seek her. She preventeth them that covet her, so that she first showeth herself unto them. He that awaketh early to seek her shall not labor, for he shall find her sitting at his door." (Wisdom vi. 13—16.) But this wisdom or love of God must be sought and asked in prayer, as St. James the Apostle writes. I am, however, far from denying that study is necessary; I wish only to say that the study of Jesus Christ crucified is more necessary.

St. Paulinus, in writing to a certain Jovian, who studied so much the writings of philosophers without caring for his progress in virtue, excusing himself by saying that he had no time, answers him : " You have time to become a philosopher, and you have none to be a Christian."

There are many students who spend almost their whole time in studying mathematics, geometry, astronomy, profane history, philosophy, etc., excusing themselves that there is no time left them for prayer and meditation. With truth, you may answer them : You have time to become a learned man and you have none to prepare yourself worthily for Holy Orders. Did not Seneca tell a great truth when he said: "We do not know what is necessary, because we learn what is surperfluous?" (De brev. irt. c. 1.) Certainly, it would be much better for a student to give up studying than to let his studies interfere with his spiritual progress.

The Apostles had received from our Lord Jesus Christ a most important mission, to go and preach the Gospel to all nations, and yet they looked upon prayer as on something more necessary and more important. Hence, when they saw that their too numerous labors interfered with this sacred duty, they chose seven Deacons, that they might do part of their work, saying : "But we will give ourselves continually to prayer, and to the ministry of the Word." (Acts vi. 4.) They say expressly, we must give ourselves first to prayer, and then only to the preaching of the Word of God, knowing very well that preaching, without prayer having preceded, would be fruitless.

St. Teresa wrote the same to the Bishop of Osma, who, for over great zeal for his flock, gave but little time to prayer and meditation. "Our Lord," writes the Saint (8th letter), "gives me to understand that you need what is most necessary—prayer and meditation, and perseverance therein, from the want of which proceeds that dryness from which your soul suffers."

St. Bernard, too, told Pope Eugene never to omit prayer for the sake of exterior occupations, as otherwise his heart might become so hardened as not even to mind any longer the stings of conscience for faults committed; nay, might become so indifferent as not to detest even faults committed. Hence St. Ignatius did not hesitate to remove many from study who could not apply to it with calmness of heart, and, therefore, found in it an obstacle to their spiritual advancement. "It may be," he said, "that they are fit for study, but study is not fit for them." "For what does it profit a man," he would say, "if he gaineth the whole world but cometh to suffer the loss of his soul." "For this end," said he, "he must always labor; everything else must be but a means tending thereto. By this principle he must be guided in all his actions." (Life by C. Genelli.)

St. Charles Borromeo made it a rule that a candidate for the priesthood should, before his ordination, be asked in particular whether he was in the habit of making his meditation, and in what manner he did it; and Father Avila, S.J., dissuaded every one from becoming a priest who was not given up to prayer.

Indeed, a student who is not fond of meditation

and prayer, will never be a good and holy priest. Whatever has been said in the preceding chapters on the necessity of prayer for all men, in order to sanctify themselves, is more justly applicable to an ecclesiastical student; for, intending, as he does, to embrace so holy a state, he is under greater obligation than the laity to sanctify himself, which he will never do without being addicted to prayer. Woe to him, should he be ordained without having given, during the course of his studies, the preference to prayer, above all his other exercises and occupations. His heart will be like a barren soil and a hard rock. Experience teaches that nothing is more apt to dry up the heart than studies without prayer. Like a sponge, they absorb all the waters of its pious sentiments and devotion. As a man attacked by cholera feels cold all over his body, so, and far more so, does a student feel in his soul, without a love for prayer. By degrees his heart becomes like a pond that has a larger outlet than inlet of water. The dry land will soon make its appearance. "He saw that the face of the earth was dried." (Genesis viii., 13.)

Studies without prayer, are, in reality, a cholera upon heart and soul. Destitute of interior light as he is, he will neither think of the necessity of sanctifying himself, nor of the obstacles thereto, and of the obligations he must comply with to save himself and others. Having no lively faith, his genuflections at the altar will be like the bows of a puppet. Could you see his interior disposition in the performance of the rites, in the administration of the sacraments, you might be tempted to believe that you saw an actor on the stage, or in the recital of his office, a harlequin going through his role. He will, as far as interior spirit and devotion are concerned, not be much unlike a bird which has been taught to sing. In preaching, he will resemble a boy reciting a lesson which he was forced to learn by heart. When speaking of the love of God, or on other virtues, he will be like a man who writes geography in his room, without having ever seen any other part of the world than his native place. In a word, the functions of his ministry, instead of being for him a source of Divine graces and benedictions, will become as many sources of maledictions; for our Lord Jesus Christ did not say in vain, "Many will say to me in that day, 'Lord, Lord, have we not prophesied in Thy Name, and cast out evils in Thy Name, and done many miracles in Thy Name,' (by administering the sacraments,) and then will I profess unto them, I never knew you; depart from Me you that work iniquity." (Matt. vii., 22.)

It is not my object to show here how far this iniquity will progress by degrees, nor to insist any longer upon the necessity of prayer for an ecclesiastical student. I content myself by saying, with Father Avila, that should he not have loved and practiced prayer in the course of his studies, he will be unfit for ordination, because he cannot possess any such solid virtue as is required for the worthy reception of Holy Orders, and as gives hopes that he will be faithful to God, "for," says St. Bernard, "if I see one not possessed of great love for prayer, I think at once to myself that there is scarcely anything good in him." "Little good," says St. Vincent de Paul, "is to be expected from a man who does not love to commune with God."

Hence St. Francis of Assisi said to St. Anthony of Padua: "I am well pleased that you teach theology to your brethren, provided you do it in such a manner that neither in you, nor in your brethren, love and fervor for prayer may be diminished." (His life.)

And St. Alphonsus wrote to the students, after the departure of a certain professor who had introduced among them a forced application to study, which very much afflicted Alphonsus, because he could not suffer it: "I am not sorry when I see you retrench your studies and give more time to prayer. We have been called to succor poor destitute souls; for this reason we have more need of sanctity than of science. If we are not holy, we are exposed to the peril of falling into a thousand imperfections. I repeat to you once more, if, to give to spirituality, you retrench some from your studies, far from being sorry, I shall, on the contrary, experience great consolation." (Life, V. vol. p. 34.)

Father John de Starchiá, Provincial of the Friars Minor in Lombardy, having been upbraided in vain by St. Francis of Assisi, for having introduced forced studies, and made regulations more favorable to science than to piety, was publicly cursed by this Saint, and deposed at the ensuing chapter. The Saint, on being entreated to withdraw this curse and give his blessing to Brother John, who was a learned nobleman, answered: "I cannot bless him whom the Lord has cursed." A dreadful reply, which was soon after verified. This unfortunate man died, exclaiming: "I am damned and cursed for all eternity." Some frightful circumstances, which followed after his death, confirmed his awful prediction. Such a malediction, which pride and disobedience, the natural consequences of neglect of prayer, brought upon this learned man, ought to strike terror into those vain men, especially those ecclesiastics who forsake piety and prayer for science, and in whom learning and talents have no other effects than to produce in them great attachment to their own conceits and proud indocility, which induces them at length even to revolt against the Church. To escape these, or similar fatal consequences, and to render themselves always more worthy of their sublime vocation, ecclesiastics must adopt the motto of St. Alphonsus, " Soli Deo et studiis," or that of Father Passerat, "D'abard l'oraison et puis l'étude;" prayer first and then study.

Hoping that none of those who read this book will belong to that class of men of whom our Lord Jesus Christ has said : " I know that My word has no place in you ;" (John viii. 37.) "And why do you not know My speech? Because you cannot hear My word ;" (Vers. xliii. 45.) " If I say the truth to you, why do you not believe Me ; he that is of God heareth the words of God, therefore you hear them not because you are not of God," I conclude by saying, that if you put in practice what has been said you will gather a large treasure of science and piety, from which, as a learned and holy scribe in the kingdom of God, you will one day "bring forth new things and old," (Matt. xiii. 52), proving yourself a faithful minister and steward, (I Cor. xiii. 8), and like a good and faithful servant, being found worthy to be placed by your Lord over many things." (Matt. xxv. 23.)

CHAPTER V.

ON THE EFFICACY OF THE PRAYER OF THE JUST.

MY dear reader, were I to ask you: 'Is there any power in the world to which God Himself submits?' Most undoubtedly you would answer: 'No; there is none, and to maintain the contrary is to incur the guilt of heresy and blasphemy.' Nevertheless, in spite of all this, I dare assert, without the slightest fear of committing the sin either of heresy or of blasphemy, that there is a power to which Almighty God feels Himself obliged to yield. 'And what is this power?' you will eagerly ask. 'It is the power of the prayer of the just.' Innumerable passages in Holy Writ, and in the lives of the Saints, prove this great truth. I have selected several for this chapter, in the hope that you will find them interesting, and that they will contribute to inflame your heart with still greater love and fervor for prayer.

We read in Exodus (c. 32, v. 10), that God was, one day, very much incensed against the Jews; for, in spite of the astounding miracles He had wrought in their behalf, when freeing them from the galling yoke of Egyptian slavery, they had fallen into the most heinous crime of idolatry. Exasperated at this most provoking offence, the Lord resolved to blot out this ungrateful people from the face of the earth. He was on the point of pouring out His wrath upon them when He desisted and refrained from giving full vent to His just indignation. Why? Because there was one to interpose and arrest His anger. Who was it? Moses. By what means did he bring about the reconciliation of God with His people? By prayer. Moses, the holy and faithful servant of God, the leader of the Israelites, interceded for them, and, by dint of earnest entreaty, arrested the arm of God uplifted to smite an ungrateful people. "Let me alone," says the Lord to Moses, "that My wrath may be kindled against them and that I may destroy them."

Behold the struggle between an angry God and His suppliant servant; between justice and prayer. "Let Me alone," ah! beloved Moses, let Me alone; let Me alone, that My wrath may be kindled against them. "Let Me alone;" do not oppose Me any longer; I will and I must take revenge; I cannot forbear any longer. "Let Me alone;" let Me execute justice; if you yield to My wish, I will make of you a great nation, i. e., the leader of another great nation. Certainly, as St. Jerome (in Ezech. c. 13) remarks, "he who says to another : 'Let me alone,' gives to understand that he is in his power, under his control!"

But Moses did not yield; on the contrary, he boldly demanded pardon of the Lord for the Jews, saying: "Why, O Lord, is Thy indignation aroused against Thy people whom Thou hast brought out of the land of Egypt, with great power and with a mighty hand? Let not the Egyptians boast, I beseech Thee: He craftily brought them out that He might kill them in the mountains and efface them from the earth: let Thy anger cease, and be appeased upon the waywardness of Thy people." What was the issue of this well-contested struggle between God and Moses? Which of the two came off victorious? Was it the Lord? No; He saw Himself subdued by the power of Moses' prayer, for "the Lord was appeased," says Holy Scripture, "from doing the evil which He had spoken against His people."

Something similar took place at the time of the prophet Jeremias. Again the Jews had committed atrocious crimes, and the wrath of the Lord was kindled anew. Again He wanted to reject and annihilate them. "And I will cast you away from before My face, as I have cast away all your brethren." (Isais. vii. 15.) But before inflicting this punishment, the Lord had to entreat His servant Jeremias not to intercede in behalf of the victims of His anger. And the Lord said to the prophet: "Therefore do not thou pray for this people, nor take to thee praise and supplication for them, and *do not withstand Me,"* (Verse 16), for if you do, the Lord means to say, I shall not be able to pour out My wrath upon this people.

Again, God visited this perverse people with a destructive fire as a chastisement for their sinful lives. Great, indeed, must have been the anger of God which obliged Him to send this frightful plague, yet still greater was the power of Aaron's prayer, since it prevailed again upon the Lord and induced Him to quench the fire immediately. Moses said to Aaron: " Take the censer, and putting fire in it from the altar, put incense upon it, and go quickly to the people to pray for them, for already wrath is gone out from the Lord and the plague rageth." (Numbers xvi. 46.) What was the result? " A blameless man (Aaron) made haste to pray for the people, bringing forth the shield of his ministry, prayer, and by incense making supplication, *withstood the wrath and put an end to the calamity, showing that he was Thy servant."* (Wisdom xviii. 21.) Thus Aaron checked this devouring flame which had already consumed fourteen thousand and seventy men, not indeed by water, but by placing himself between the living and the dead, offering fervent prayer to the Lord. " And standing between the dead and the living, he prayed for the people and the plague ceased." (Num. xvi. 48.)

At the time of the deluge, Noah became the reconciler of man with God, as we read in the Book of

Ecclesiasticus, chap. xliv. 17, God, for his sake, putting an end to the deluge, and saving in him and his family the whole human race. "Noah was found perfect, just." Hence it was that he could appease the wrath of God: "And in the time of wrath he was made a reconciliation."

What made Attila, the scourge of God, retreat so suddenly and give up his plan of invading Italy? It was the prayer of St. Leo, Pope, in deference to which God sent so great a consternation upon Attila that he felt himself forced to withdraw. What put an effectual check to the ravages of pestilence at the time of St. Gregory? Nothing but the prayers of this Saint. What terminated the persecutions of the ten Roman emperors? Was it not the prayer of St. Silvester, who healed, converted, and baptized Constantine the Great? Do we not come across similar examples in almost all the lives of the Saints? The hands of God are, then, so to speak, bound by the prayer of men eminently just, but He feels free to act if such men cannot be found. As He Himself declared by the prophet Ezechiel: (chap. xxii. 30.) "And I sought among them a man that might set up a hedge and stand in the gap before Me in favor of the land, that I might not destroy it; and I found none. And I poured out My indignation upon them; in the fire of My wrath I consumed them."

The terrible fate of Sodom, as related in the Book
11

of Genesis, is an evident proof of this truth. No sooner had Abraham learned that God intended to destroy this city with its inhabitants, than he commenced to intercede for it, saying to the Lord: " Wilt Thou destroy the just with the wicked ? If there be fifty just men in the city, shall they perish withal ? and wilt Thou not spare that place for the sake of the fifty just, if they be therein ? Far be it from Thee to do this thing, and to slay the just with the wicked, and for the just to be in like case with the wicked, this is not beseeming Thee : Thou Who judgest all the earth, wilt not make this judgment." And the Lord said to him: " If I find in Sodom fifty just within the city, I will spare the whole place for their sake." And Abraham answered and said : Seeing I have once begun, I will speak to my Lord, whereas I am dust and ashes. What if there be five less than fifty just persons ? Wilt Thou for five and forty destroy the whole city ? And He said : I will not destroy it if I find five and forty. And again he said to Him : But if forty be found there what wilt Thou do ? He said : I will not destroy it for the sake of forty. Lord, saith he, be not angry, I beseech Thee, if I speak : What if thirty shall be found there ? He answered, " I will not do it if I find thirty there." "Seeing," saith he, " I have once begun, I will speak to my Lord." " What if twenty be found there ? He said : I will not destroy it for the sake of twenty. I beseech

Thee, saith he, be not angry Lord, if I speak yet once more: What if ten should be found there? And he said, I will not destroy it for the sake of ten." (Gen. xviii. 23-32.) And the Lord departed, fearing, as it were, Abraham might ask Him to spare the city if but four, or three, or even one just soul could be found there; for there was that number to be found there, viz: Lot, his wife and two children. But in order that they might not perish with the rest, God, through the ministry of his angels, led them out of the city. But had the Lord found there but ten just men, surely He would have spared the city. Nay, at the time of Jeremias, God declared, through his prophet, that He would be propitious to the city of Jerusalem, if but one just man could be found therein. "Go about through the streets of Jerusalem and see, and consider, and seek in the broad places thereof if you can find a man that executeth judgment and seeketh faith, *and I will be merciful unto it.*' (Chap. v. 1.) God seeks men to whom may be applied what is said of St. John the Baptist: " He was great before the Lord," that is, great with God by their holiness of life, and great by the power of their prayer.

Such was St. Athanasius, who for God and for the sake of religion, opposed the dreadful heresy of Arius and triumphed over it. Such was St. John Chrysostom, St. Basil, St. Augustine, St. Ambrose, who, to the end of their lives, fought the battles of the Lord. In what great esteem must the just be held, though despicable and wretched exteriorly, because, for their sake, God spares whole cities sunk in vice; they are the stays and pillars of realms. Such was David, of whom God said to Ezechias : I will protect this city and will save it for My own sake, and *for David My servant's sake.*" (IV. Kings xix. 34.)

Such was St. Paul, to whom, when in danger of shipwreck, the Angel of the Lord said : " Fear not, Paul, for thou must be brought before Cæsar ; and behold, God hath given thee all that sail with thee." (Acts xxvii. 24.) Hence Cornelius a Lapide remarks: " God values one just man more than a thousand sinners, than heaven and earth ;" " nay," says St. Alphonsus, "God esteems one eminently just man more than a thousand ordinary just men. As one sun imparts more light and warmth to the whole world than all the stars united, in like manner a holy man benefits the world more than a thousand ordinary just men." " Who will call into doubt that the world is sustained by the prayers of the Saints," says Ruff. Praefat. in vit. Patr.

On this account, St. Gregory writes : " Oh, how I am grieved to the very heart, when I see that God banishes holy men and women from one country into another, or summons them to Himself. This is to me an evident sign that He intends to punish such a country, and it will be, indeed, very easy for

Him, when there is no one left to stay His anger." Hence St. Augustine was right in saying : "The prayer of the just man is a key to heaven ; let his prayer ascend and God's mercy will descend." (Serm. 226 de Tempore.)

All the just men, of the Old and the New Testament, employed this key of prayer very freely to unlock God's inexhaustible treasures, and to obtain for themselves and others whatever blessing they needed, whether temporal or spiritual. With this key the prophet Elias closed the heavens, and no rain fell for three years and a half; and with this same key he opened them again, and again rain fell in abundance. With this key Ezechias brought back the shadow of the lines by which it was gone down in the sun-dial of Achaz, with the sun ten lines backwards. " And the sun returned ten lines by the degrees by which it was gone down." (Isais. xxxviii. 8.)

With this key also, Josue arrested the sun in its course, to have a longer day for gaining a complete victory over the Amorrhites : " Move not, O sun, towards Gabaon, nor thou, O moon, towards the valley of Ajalon." (Josue x. 12.) What happened? "And the sun and the moon stood still, till the people revenged themselves of their enemies. So the sun stood still in the midst of heaven, and hastened not to go down the space of one day. There was not before nor after so long a day, *the*

11*

Lord obeying the voice of a man." (Verse 13.)
Thus Josue exercises power over the heavenly planets, suspending their revolutions, as if king thereof, and keeping them at his beckon.

With the key of prayer Jacob, the Nisibite, keeps the gates of Nisibis closed against Sapor, and sets all his schemes at naught, as Theodore writes in this Abbot's life; Bessarion, the Abbot, turns sea water into sweet water; St. Raymond of Pennafort, standing on his mantle, traverses the sea for a distance of one hundred and sixty miles; the Monk Publius prevented Azazel, Julian the Apostate's devil (dispatched by this impious emperor to bring news from the Occident, as is related in Vitis. Pat. lib. 6, tome. 2, No. 12), from proceeding farther west than where he lived; St. Hilarion, Macarius, and other Saints, drove out the devil from possessed persons; Theonas, the Abbot, made robbers stand immovable; St. Gregory Thaumaturgas moves a mountain to obtain a site for a church; St. Francis of Assisium renders a wolf quite tame and gentle; St. Alphonsus stems a lava-torrent of Mount Vesuvius, and turns its destructive course from the city of Naples; St. Stanislaus, the Martyr, restores a man to life who had died three years before, and presented him before the court, to testify that he had bought a certain spot, as a situation for his church, from him, and had paid him in full.

"My dear Lord," says St. Coletta, after the

death of her Prior, "give me back my Prior, for I need his aid still in erecting some more monasteries," and our Lord is pleased to restore this Saint, her Prior, alive, and he rendered valuable services during the fifteen years he lived afterwards.

St. Francis de Paul, learning that his parents were to be executed for the supposed murder of a man, whose body had been found in their garden, says to our Lord: "My God, let me be with my parents by to-morrow." In the same night he was carried by an Angel to his parents, at a distance of four hundred leagues. The next day he commands the dead man, in the presence of the people, to declare whether the murder had been justly laid to the charge of his parents. "No," says he, "your parents are guiltless." The Saint again says to the Lord: "Lord, return me to my convent," and the Angel bore him back again.

Ah! how powerful is the prayer of the just! It not only exercises its power over all kinds of creatures, rational and irrational; over those in heaven, on earth and under the earth; it not only disarms the wrath of God against entire nations, lost to the fear and love of their Creator; it exercises a mightier sway; it gives free access to the spiritual treasures of God; it causes them to flow in perpetual streams upon sinners, as well as upon the just, operating wonders in their interior. Sinners, from being enemies of God, become His friends;

from being reprobates, they become chosen vessels of election ; from being children of the devil, they become children of God ; from being heirs of hell, they become heirs of heaven.

Now, if prayer opens to sinners the road to heaven, if it produces such wonderful effects in their souls, how much more wonderful are the transformations which it brings about in the souls of the just? To give a full and accurate description of them is utterly impossible ; no human eye ever saw them, nor did any human understanding ever fully comprehend them. Could they be seen or understood, the whole world would covet them, and regard all else as vanity and unworthy of man's ambition.

Now let me enumerate some of these wonderful effects. Innumerable are the evil tendencies from which the sacred waters of baptism could not free the soul ; then, the slight blemishes which tarnish the soul, even after the remission of grievous sins in the sacrament of penance, such as temporal punishments due to every actual sin, a certain lassitude, inconstancy and discouragement in combatting the temptations of the devil, the world and the flesh ; a certain proneness and affection for the vanities of life, a sovereign horror for suffering, contempt and the like. Prayer removes these blemishes, according to what St. John Chrysostom tells us. "Although we may be filled with sins, yet, if we continue to pray, we shall soon be quite free of them;" that is to say, not only free of sins themselves, but also of temporal punishments due to them; "for," continues the Saint, "no sooner had the leper prostrated himself at the feet of our Lord, than he felt completely cleansed of his leprosy."

In prayer God enlightens the soul the better to know and understand the enormity and heinousness of sin and its ingratitude towards God. If, in the first instant of conversion, its sorrow proceeded from the imperfect motives of having lost heaven and deserved hell, it now commences to repent more from the perfect motive of the love of God, Whom, instead of offending, it should have endeavored to love above all things. It sometimes weeps over its offenses offered to God, and sheds tears of gratitude towards Him, Who, instead of punishing it in hell, gives it still time for tears and penance; its will soon conceives such a hatred of sin, that the very name of this evil will inspire it with horror. Hence, the soul's generous resolve rather to undergo every loss, even that of life itself, than to commit again the least fault; it will become penetrated with the spirit of penance, ready to accept every trial and cross as a satisfaction for its sins, an effect of the love of God increasing in it in proportion to its perseverance and fervor in prayer. "The love of God," says St. Ambrose, "having once entered into a soul, is like a fire, destroying everything that comes within its reach ; the love of God, in like manner, effaces every spot and stain of sin in the soul." Witness the good thief on the cross, who heard these consoling words from the lips of our Lord, as a response to his earnest petition, " To-day thou shalt be with Me in Paradise." Moreover, prayer inspires the soul with courage to combat all her enemies, and patiently to endure every cross and trial. She was weak, now she is strong ; she was indolent and slothful, now she is assiduous and watchful; from being perplexed, she becomes enlightened ; from being melancholy and cast down, she becomes joyful ; from being effeminate, she becomes manful. From the tower of prayer Esther comes forth courageous to brave the orders of Assuerus ; Judith faces Holofernes ; a small number of the Machabees set their numerous enemies at defiance. Fortified by prayer, our Lord Jesus Christ went to meet His enemies, who were to crucify Him.

In prayer the soul is raised above itself, to its God in heaven, where it learns, nay, even sees the vanity of all earthly things, despising them as mere trifles. There it learns that only in heaven true riches, honors and pleasures are to be found. " If we give ourselves up to prayer," says St. John Chrysostom, " we shall soon cease to be mortals, not, indeed, by nature, but by our manner of thinking, speaking, and acting, which will be divine, having, as it were, already passed to eternal life ; for those who enter into familiarity with God, must necessarily be raised above everything transitory and perishable." And again: "How great a dignity is it not, to be allowed to converse with God? By prayer we are united to the angelic choirs, who, lost in the contemplation of God, teach us how to forget ourselves whilst at prayer, so that, being penetrated with seraphic happiness and reverential awe at the same time, we may be lost to everything earthly, believing ourselves standing in the midst of the Angels, and offering with them the same sacrifice. How great is the wisdom, how great the piety, how great the holiness, how great the temperance, with which prayer fills us! Hence, it is not the slightest deviation from truth to maintain that prayer is the source of all virtues, so much so that nothing tending to nourish piety can enter the soul without its practice. (Lib. 2, de orando.)

In prayer the soul becomes aware how all the crosses and sufferings of this world, poverty, sickness, hunger and thirst, privations of all kinds, persecutions, contempt, mockeries, insults, and whatever may be repugnant to human nature and abhorred by it, is to be made light of, and, according to St. Paul, " are not worthy to be compared with the glory to come, that shall be revealed in us," (Rom. viii., 18,) exclaiming with St. Andrew, the Apostle, " O, thou good cross, which hast received thy splendor from the members of Jesus Christ, for which I have been sighing so long, which I have always loved so ardently, and which finally has been prepared for me, O, come and restore me to my Master, in order that I may be received by Him through thee, by which He was pleased to redeem me."

Hence we read that the first Christians and many martyrs would suffer with joy the loss of all their temporal goods, even life itself. I cannot refrain from relating here what one of our Fathers told me of a priest of eighty years old, with whom he had one day the happiness to dine. Whilst sitting at table he noticed protuberances of flesh on each side of the aged Father's hands. Not knowing how to account for them, he asked for an explanation. The venerable old priest told him that when the slaughter of priests was going on by wholesale, during the French revolution, he tried to escape death by hiding himself in a rack of hay. An officer, probing the rack with his sword, pierced the hay and his hands at the same time, which were lying crosswise, thus discovering him and taking him to prison, to be executed on the next day. "Never in my life," said he, "did I experience such agony, such deadly fear; never did I understand more clearly what our dear Lord suffered in the garden of Gethsemane, than I did at that time. According to the example of my Divine Redeemer, I commenced to pray, and prayed until three o'clock in the morning. Suddenly I felt so great a comfort, consolation and courage that I even sighed after the hour of my execution. Would to God they came, I exclaimed with a sigh. Would to God they came! At last the door of the prison is thrown open. There they are, I said; thanks be to God, now I am going to die for Jesus Christ. But, alas! my exceedingly great joy is, in an instant, changed into an excess of grief. I was told that I was not to be executed, but set at liberty." Thus, prayer changed this priest's sadness into joy, his cowardice into intrepidity, his horror of torture into a longing desire for the most exquisite torments.

Prayer, moreover, unites the soul to God in an indescribably wonderful manner. This union is much stronger, more solid, more intimate than the best kind of cement is capable of producing between two stones. Physical force can separate the latter; the former is incapable of dissolution by any natural power whatever. As fire seems to change iron into fire, the sun to change the air into light, in like manner the soul becomes penetrated with God in prayer. "But he who is joined to the Lord," says St. Paul, "is one spirit." (1 Cor. vi., 17.) To be given up to prayer, and to be joined to God, is one and the same thing—the soul becoming with God one spirit, one will. "For," says St. John Chrysostom, "if he who converses frequently with a great and conspicuous personage must necessarily draw from this intercourse the greatest advantages, how much more abundant must be the blessings flowing from the constant communion with God! As one who frequently enjoys the company of a wise, prudent and learned man, whom he truly loves and esteems, will, by degrees, adopt his manners and his way of speaking, judging and acting; so a soul which converses often and long with God in prayer, will gradually receive more and more of the divine attributes, exchanging, so to speak, her own will for that of God. St. Bernard expresses himself most beautifully and just to the point when he says: "Such a one not only wishes what God wishes, nay, the disposition of his will is such that it cannot wish except what God wishes; but to wish what God wishes is already to be like unto God; now not to be able to will anything save what God wills, is to be what God is, with Whom to will and to be is but one and the same. Hence it is said with truth that we shall see Him then such as He is. Now, if we have thus become like unto Him, we shall be what He Himself is; for to whomsoever power is given to become the children of God, power is also given, not, indeed, to be God themselves, but to be what God is." (St. Bern. or Auct. tract de vita solitar, towards the end.)

Hence, St. Francis of Assisium, when at prayer, was oftentimes wrapped in ecstacy, and, regardless of earth and the love of created things, he would exclaim, in a transport of delight: "My God and my all! My God and my all! Let me die for the love of Thee Who hast died for the love of me!"

Hence that brilliant light ever beaming on the countenances of holy men when returning from fervent prayer and familiar intercourse with God. "And when Moses came down from Mount Sinai . . . . . he knew not that his face was horned from the conversation of the Lord." (Exodus xxxiv., 29.)

Those who are devoted to prayer and frequent conversation with God become like Moses, whose brow was resplendent with a supernatural light. This brilliancy is first visible on their countenance, and then extends to the whole body. Thus Jesus Christ was transfigured in prayer, and His face did shine as the sun, so much so that this light not only reflected upon Moses and Elias, but also upon St. Peter, St. James and St. John, in which light St. Peter, inebriated with joy, exclaims: " Lord, it is good for us to be here ; if Thou wilt let us make here three tabernacles, one for Thee, and one for Moses, and one for Elias."

Thus the face of St. Anthony, who often spent whole nights in prayer, would be resplendent to such a degree that by the splendor, radiance, and joy on his countenance, he could be recognized at once among many thousands of his brethren, not unlike a sun among many stars ; thus, too, St. Francis of Assisium would shine, whilst elevated in spirit to heaven in the act of fervent prayer, so much so that he seemed to send forth fiery flames. In the Breviary, we read of St. Stanislaus Koska that his face was always inflamed, nay, sometimes even beaming with divine light.

Thus, also, the countenance of the Blessed Virgin Mary shone constantly, and in an especial manner, with heavenly light, on account of her perpetual union with God and the Incarnate Word, and such was its dazzling splendor that, according to the testimony of St. Dionysius, the Areopagite, she seemed to be a goddess.

Now, these beams radiated in the shape of horns to signify that the Saints were not only enlightened in prayer, but became also cornuti-horned, i. e., constant, firm, strong, intrepid, and capable of undergoing every suffering, and of enduring all kinds of hardships.

Thus Anna, the mother of Samuel, felt great strength and courage after her prayer, according to what is related of her: (I Kings, i. 18.) "And her countenance was no more changed." that is, from that very moment she received, with an even and constant mind, both the praises of Helcana and the contempt and mockery of Phenanna, consolations and prosperity as well as desolations and adversities.

Finally, prayer introduces the soul into that happy country of the interior life, a country overflowing with milk and honey. Here the soul learns more of God in one moment than by reading all the books ever written; God speaks to the soul and the soul to God in an inexplicable manner, enkindling her with that strong, ardent and seraphic love for Himself which made St. Paul exclaim: "Who, then, shall separate us from the love of Christ? shall tribulations? or distress? or famine? or nakedness? or danger? or persecution? or the sword? as it is written, For Thy sake we are put to death all the day long. We are accounted as sheep for the slaughter." (Rom. viii. 35.) "Even unto this hour we both hunger and thirst, and are naked, and are buffeted, and have no fixed abode. We are reviled, ... We are persecuted, ... we are blasphemed; we are made as the refuse of this world, the offscouring of all even until now." (Corinth. iv. 11—13.) "Our flesh had no rest, but we suffered all tribulation; combats without; fears within;" (II Corinth. vii. 5,) "in many labors, in prisons more frequently, in stripes above measure, in deaths often. Of the Jews five times did I receive forty stripes, save one. Thrice was I beaten with rods, once I was stoned, thrice I suffered shipwreck; a night and a day I was in the depths of the sea. In journeying often in perils of water, in perils of robbers, in perils from my own nation, in perils from the gentiles, in perils in the city, in perils in the wilderness, in perils in the sea, in perils from false brethren, in labor and painfulness, in much watchings, in hunger and thirst, in fastings often, in cold and in nakedness." (II Cor. xi. 23-28.) "We glory in tribulations." (Rom. v. 3;) "I am filled with comfort; I exceedingly bound with joy in all our tribulations." (II Cor. vii. 4.) "In all these things we overcome, because of Him that hath loved us. For I am sure that neither death, nor life, nor Angels, nor principalities, nor powers, nor things present, nor things to come, nor might, nor height, nor depth, nor any other creature, shall be able to separate us from the love of God, which is in Christ Jesus our Lord." (Rom. viii. 37—39.)

What is there still that cannot be obtained through prayer. "All things whatsoever you shall ask in prayer, believing, you shall receive." (Matt. xxi. 22.) Now, he who says all things, excepts nothing. Nay, God is so good, so liberal, says Origen, (hom. 9, in Numer.) that He gives more than He is asked for. The Holy Church, too, expresses this when she prays: "Oh, God, Who, in the abundance of Thy kindness, *exceedest both the merits and wishes of Thy suppliants*, pour forth upon us Thy mercy that Thou mayst free us from those things which burden our conscience, and mayst grant us what we dare not ask."

Let us add a word in conclusion : He who understands how to pray well becomes, as it were, the lord of the Lord, and the ruler of the universe. He is another Jacob, who, having overcome the Lord in wrestling, (in prayer) was called Israel, i. e., the conqueror of God. By praying to God he becomes Israel, "the victor of God." Hence Cornelius a Lapide remarks: "If you can reason with God effectually in prayer, your enemies will, at once, become your friends or your subjects, God so changing them."

This secret of conquering, and this manner of obtaining whatever they wished, has always been known and adopted up to the present day by holy souls, who enjoy the intimate friendship of God, through Whom they do wondrous things. "I can do," says St. Paul, "all things in Him Who strengthens me," for the hearts even of the most ferocious are in the hands of the Lord Who changes them at His good pleasure. "If thou 'hast been strong against God, how much more shalt thou prevail against men." (Gen. xxxii. 28.) Indeed, whomsoever the Creator Himself obeys, the Angels, the demons, men, and all creatures, are bound to obey.

CHAPTER VI.

ON THE CONDITIONS AND QUALITIES OF PRAYER.

PLUTARCH relates that, in his time, the Romans sent a delegation of three men to Bithynia, in order to restore peace between a father and his son. One of the delegates had his head covered with ulcers; the other suffered from gout, and the third from heart disease. When Cato, the Roman Censor, saw them, he exclaimed: "This Roman delegation has neither head, nor foot, nor heart." I fear, dear reader, that we often send similar worthless delegations to God. Our delegate to Him is prayer, of which David has said: "Let my prayer come before Thee;" (Ps. lxxxvii. 3) on which words St. Augustine comments thus: "O wonderful power of prayer, which has access to God, whilst the flesh is refused admittance." Now, in order that our delegate may please God and prove as useful and powerful to us as it has to the Saints, it must have certain conditions and qualities; above all,

I.—The Object of our Prayer must be Lawful.

Were we to pray for anything which it is unlawful for us to desire, our request would be rash or indiscreet, as for instance:
1. If we petition for what might be detrimental to our salvation. "A man," says St. Augustine, "may lawfully pray for the necessities of this life, and the Lord may mercifully refuse to hear him. As a physician, who desires the restoration of his patient, will not allow him those things which he knows will be hurtful to him—or as a mother ought not to give a knife to her little child, although he should ask for it, so, in like manner, our Lord will turn a deaf ear to our prayers when we ask for such things as He knows it would be inexpedient to grant. Hence, sometimes a person's prayer for temporal favors is refused, because God foresees the injury they would do that person. For this reason St. Philip Neri would pray only conditionally for sick persons, because several of those, who had recovered their health by his prayers, had relapsed into their former excesses, and led very licentious lives. It is, however, not forbidden to pray for the necessaries of life, as Solomon did: "Give me only the necessaries of life;" (Prov. xxx. 8.) nor is it wrong to be solicitous about such things, provided our anxiety with regard to them

be not inordinate, and we do not set our hearts upon them so absolutely as to make them the chief objects of our desires. We must always ask for them with resignation, and with the condition that they be of advantage to our souls. We read in the Life of St. Thomas of Canterbury, that a sick man, who had recovered his health through the Saint's intercession, reflecting afterwards that sickness might have been better for him than health, he prayed again to the holy Bishop, saying, that he would prefer being sick, if health was not desirable for him, and immediately his sickness returned.

2. If we pray to be delivered from a particular temptation, or cross, (as St. Paul prayed for deliverance from the temptations of the flesh) which God knows to be useful to our advancement in humility and other virtues.

3. If we ask for something from motives of ambition, like the sons of Zebedee, who prayed to obtain the principal offices in the kingdom of Christ.

4. If we ask for something from indiscreet zeal, like the Apostles when they asked our Lord to send down fire from heaven upon the Samaritans, because they rejected Christ our Lord.

5. If we ask for something, the granting of which God delays for some time for our profit, in order to increase our zeal and fervor in prayer, and enable us to merit the virtue of perseverance. One

day St. Gertrude complained to our Lord because she had not obtained from Him a certain favor for her relatives, notwithstanding His promise to her to hear all her prayers. Our Lord answered her that He had heard her prayer, but would grant the favor asked at some future period when it would be more useful to her relatives.

6. And especially if we were to ask of God a certain particular state of life, as the sacerdotal, religious, or matrimonial, and He in His Omniscience knowing that we would be more easily saved or obtain more merit in a different state better suited to our physical, intellectual, and moral constitution. The appropriate prayer in such a case is daily to beseech the Almighty to direct us by such means and ways as will secure us from sin, make us more holy, and lead us to life everlasting, saying: " Lord what wilt Thou have me to do." " My heart is ready, O God, my heart is ready." " Show, O Lord, Thy ways to me, and teach me Thy paths." (Ps. xxiv. 4.) " As we know not, O Lord, what to do, we can only turn our eyes to Thee." (II Paral. xx. 12.) " Guide me, O Lord, by those ways, offices, actions, exercises and sufferings, which Thou knowest will lead me most safely to Paradise ; and to greater glory in Thy heavenly kingdom." Many persons are accustomed also to pray thus : " Grant, O Lord, what Jesus Christ, my Redeemer Himself, wishes to see in me ; and what He wills should be

given to me ; and what, when dying on the cross, He asked for me." Or : Grant me, O Lord, what the Blessed Virgin Mary wishes me, and what she herself asks for me, for she loves me and wishes to see me saved, and knows best what I need to obtain eternal happiness. This is a very pious and most efficacious manner of praying.

7. If our prayers are said, as it were, at random, without asking any particular grace, they are also more or less defective, indiscreet, and inefficacious. "You know not what you ask ;" (Mark x. 38.) said our Lord Jesus Christ to the sons of Zebedee when they asked of Him that they might sit, one on His right hand and the other on His left hand, in His glory. Alas, how many Christians there are to whom our Lord could address the same words, you do not know what you ask of God. How many are there who, if they were asked on their way to church, or during their stay therein, or on their return, what they want or sought to obtain in their prayers, would be at a loss for an answer ; not knowing what they need nor what to ask for. It is self-deception to go to the Altar and pray and converse with God, asking something at random. Like a person who is sick and goes to a druggist to buy medicine without reflecting whether or not it will suit his particular disease. Such a manner of praying is certainly injudicious, because it is not adapted to the spiritual wants of our souls. Hence, we must

see that our prayers be so constituted as to correspond to our particular necessities. "When at prayer," says St. Francis de Sales, "let us be like a strong, robust, and sensible man, who, when sitting at table takes such food as will give him bodily strength, and not like children who grasp at sweet things, such as sugar, cakes, pears, apples and the like." Prayer is called the food of the soul, but it is so only when we pray according to its spiritual wants.

8. If we pray in too general a manner, for example, should a person from certain circumstances in life, either from necessity or otherwise, be thrown into the society of another of a quarrelsome, irritable, dissatisfied disposition, he would naturally desire not to lose patience or become angry, or use uncharitable words or reproaches. Should he pray thus to God: "Lord, give me patience, make me humble and charitable;" this prayer might be considered rather too general and indefinite. It would be better to say: "Lord, make me patient and charitable towards this person, give me also the grace to have immediate recourse to Thee, whenever ill feelings commence to arise in my heart, at that very moment make me pray that I may have strength to resist them for the love of Thee." It is not here intended to convey the idea that to pray in a general manner for our wants is not good, but only that it is better to pray according to the particular circumstances of our wants.

9. There is yet another mode of praying in use with many persons not very profitable to the soul, and is, therefore, more or less inexpedient; it is to pray by way of affections, for instance, " O, excess of love! One heart is too little to love Thee, my Jesus; one tongue is not enough to praise Thy goodness. O, my Jesus, how great are my obligations to Thee! No, I will no longer live in myself, but that Jesus alone should live in me, He is mine and I am His. O love! O love! No more sins! I will never forget the goodness of God and the mercies of my Saviour. I love Thee, O Infinite Majesty; my God, I wish to love nothing but Thee," &c.

Expressions like these are called devout affections of the heart; but, as they do not contain the least petition for any particular grace, the soul will not become over rich with the gifts of God if this manner of praying be adopted. If a beggar were to say to a millionaire: " Oh, how magnificent is your house; how splendid your furniture; how elegant your grounds; how vast your wealth, it would hardly excite the rich man to almsgiving." But should he say: " My good sir, be kind enough to assist me in my poverty; please give me some money, some clothes, some provisions," &c., then the man of wealth, if charitably disposed, would hardly fail to give him what he asked for. In like manner our Lord is not bound to bestow graces upon us because we admire His perfections, goodness or other attributes. But if we say to Him: "Lord, give me to understand better the excess of Thy love; grant that my heart may never love anything but Thee, that it may ever be Thine; make me always seek only Thee; let everything else be distasteful to me," &c., expressions like these being petitions or prayers, in which we ask for particular graces, our Lord Jesus Christ, on account of His promise, feels bound to grant them. Although devout affections are good, and often quite natural to the soul, yet, generally speaking, petitions are better, far more profitable, and more conformable to the examples taught us by our Lord Jesus Christ, the Holy Church in her authorized devotions, and all the Saints. Read the prayer of our Lord for His disciples in the Gospel of St. John (chap. 17), or any prayer of the Church, or of any Saint, and the truth of this can be seen. Refer to a prayer of St. Alphonsus Liguori, justly termed the Apostle of Prayer, to our Lord in the Blessed Sacrament, commencing: "Oh, my Jesus, Thou Who art the true life, make me die to the world to live only to Thee; my Redeemer, by the flames of Thy love destroy all in me that is displeasing to Thee, and give me a true desire to gratify and please Thee in all things," &c.

The Ven. Paul Segneri used to say that, at one time, he used to employ the time of prayer in reflections and affections, "but God (these are his own words), afterwards opened my eyes, and thenceforward I endeavored to occupy my time with petitions ; and if there is any good in me, I ascribe it to this exercise of recommending myself to God." Let us likewise do the same. And it may not be out of place to suggest that, in the selection of a Prayer-Book, one in which the prayers are in the form of petitions, is the most profitable.

Certain persons having heard or read, in the lives of St. Teresa and other Saints, of the grades of supernatural prayer, namely, the prayer of quiet, of sleep, or suspension of the faculties, of union, of ecstacy or rapture, of flight and impetus of the spirit, and of the wound of love, may feel anxious to possess, and even pray fervently for these supernatural gifts. The learned and pious Palafox, Bishop of Osma, in a note on the 18th letter of St. Teresa, says : "Observe that these supernatural graces which God deigned to bestow on St. Teresa, and other Saints, are not necessary for the attainment of sanctity, since, without them, many have arrived at a high degree of perfection, and obtained eternal life, while many who enjoyed them were afterwards damned." He says that "the practice of the Gospel virtues, and particularly of the love of God, being the true and only way to sanctify our souls, it is superfluous, and even presumptuous, to desire and seek such extraordinary gifts." These virtues are acquired by prayer, and by corresponding with the lights and helps of God, Who ardently desires our sanctification: "For this is the will of God, your sanctification." (Thess. iv. 3.)

Speaking of the degrees of supernatural prayer described by St. Teresa, the holy Bishop wisely observes that, "as to the prayer of *quiet*, we should only desire and beg of God to free us from all attachment and affection to worldly goods, which, instead of giving peace to the soul, fill it with inquietude and affliction. Solomon justly called them "vanity of vanities, and vexation of spirit." (Eccl. i. 14.)

"The heart of man can never enjoy true peace till it is divested of all that is not God, and entirely devoted to His holy love, to the exclusion of every other object. But man himself cannot attain to this perfect consecration of his being to God; he can only obtain it by constant prayer. As to the *sleep* or *suspension of the powers*, we should entreat the Almighty to keep them in a profound sleep with regard to all temporal affairs and awake only to meditate on His Divine goodness, and to seek Divine love and eternal goods. For all sanctity, and the perfection of charity, consist in the union of our will with the holy will of God. As to *union of the powers*, we should only pray that God may teach us by His grace, not to think of, or seek, or wish for anything but what He wills. As to *ecstacy* or *rapture*, let us beseech the Lord to eradicate from our hearts all inordinate love of ourselves and of creatures, and to draw us entirely to Himself. As to the *flight of the spirit*, we should merely implore the grace of perfect detachment from the world, that, like the swallow which never seeks its food on the earth, and even feeds in its flight, we may never fix our heart on any sensual enjoyment, but, always tending towards heaven, employ the goods of this world only for the support of life. As to the *impulse of spirit*, let us ask of God courage and strength to do that violence to ourselves which may be necessary to resist the attacks of the enemy, to overcome our passions, or to embrace sufferings even in the midst of spiritual dryness and desolation. Finally, as to the *wound of love*, as the remembrance of a wound is constantly kept alive by the pain it inflicts, so we should supplicate our Lord to wound our hearts with holy love to such a degree that we may be always reminded of His goodness and affection towards us, that thus we may devote our lives to love and please Him by our works and affections. These graces will not be obtained without prayer, but by humble, confident and persevering prayer, all the gifts of God may be procured." Let us, then, always pray the Lord to hear us, not, indeed, according to our will, but rather to grant us what may be conducive to our sanctification and salvation. Let us not be like the blind man in the Gospel, whom our Saviour asked, "What wilt thou that I do to thee." (Luke xviii. 41.) "Indeed," says St. Bernard, "this man was truly blind, God finding it necessary to ask him what He should do to him ; he should have said : Lord, be it far from me that Thou shouldst do to me according to my will ; no, do to me according to Thy will, and what Thou knowest is best for me." St. Jerome writes, in his letter to Salvian, that Nebridius was in the habit of asking of God to give him what He knew was most suitable for him. Hence St. John says: "This is the confidence which we have towards God, that whatsoever we shall ask, *according to His will*, He heareth us." (I. John, v. 14.)

Such was the prayer of Solomon. "And the Lord appeared to Solomon . . . . . saying : Ask what thou wilt that I should give thee. And Solomon said : . . . . O, Lord God, Thou hast made Thy servant king, instead of David, my father, and I am but a child, and know not how to go out and come in, ... give, therefore, Thy servant an understanding heart . . . to *discern between good and evil*. And the Lord said to Solomon : Because thou hast asked this thing, and hast not asked for thyself long life, nor riches, nor the lives of thy enemies, but has asked *for thyself wisdom to discern judgment, behold, I have done for thee according to thy words*, and have given thee a wise and understanding heart, insomuch that there has been no one like thee before thee, nor shall arise after thee. Yea, and the things also which thou didst not ask, I have given thee, to-wit, riches and glory, so that no one hath been like thee among the kings in all days heretofore." (III. Kings iii., 5, 6, 7, 14.)

Solomon is called the "Wise Man," and, indeed, he manifested great wisdom in his prayer to God ; so much so that the Lord praised him for it, and granted him not only what he asked, but even far more than he could expect. Let us pray like him, saying : "Lord, I am living in a wicked world, surrounded with dangers, which lead to perdition. I am like a child, not knowing how to walk or to follow the true way. Give, therefore, to Thy servant an understanding heart to discern between good and evil. Make me understand what a great evil sin is, and what a great good it is to love Thee above all things. Give me a great hatred to sin, and make me love Thee most ardently to the end of my life."

Or, let us pray like St. Francis of Assisium : "Our Father," most blessed, most holy, our Creator, Redeemer, and Comforter ; "Who art in heaven ;" where Thou dwellest with the Angels and the Saints, whom Thou enlightenest and inflamest with Thy love so that they may know Thee ; for Thou, O Lord, art the life and love that dwell in them ; Thou art their everlasting happiness, communicating Thyself to them: Thou art the supreme and eternal source from which all blessings flow, and without Thee there is none ; "Hallowed be Thy name ;" enlighten us with Thy Divine Wisdom, that we may be able to know Thee and to comprehend the boundless extent of Thy mercies to us, Thy everlasting promises, Thy sublime majesty, and Thy profound judgments; "Thy kingdom come ;" so that Thy grace may reign in our hearts, and prepare us for Thy heavenly kingdom, where we shall see Thee clearly and perfectly love Thee, rejoicing with Thee and in Thee through all eternity ; " Thy will be done on earth as it is in heaven ;" that being occupied with Thee we may love Thee with our whole heart ; with our whole soul, desiring nothing but Thee, with our whole mind, referring all things to Thee, and ever seeking Thy glory in all our actions, with our whole strength, employing all our faculties, both of body and soul in Thy service, applying them to no other end whatsoever than to promote Thy kingdom, seeking to draw all men to Thee, and to love our neighbor as ourselves, rejoicing at his welfare and happiness as if it were our own, sympathizing with his necessities and giving no offence to him ; " Give us this day our daily bread ;" Thy dearly beloved Son, our Lord Jesus Christ, we ask Him of Thee as our daily bread, in order that we may be mindful of the love

He testified for us and of the things He promised, did, and suffered for us ; grant us the grace always to keep them in our thoughts, and to value them exceedingly ; " Forgive us our trespasses ;" through Thy unspeakable mercy, through the merits of the passion and death of Thy most dearly beloved Son, through the intercession of the Holy Virgin Mary, and of all the Saints ; " As we forgive them that trespass against us ;" grant us the grace that we may sincerely and truly forgive our enemies, and pray earnestly to Thee for them ; that we may never return evil for evil, but seek to do good to those who injure us ; " And lead us not into temptation ;" whether it be concealed, manifest, or sudden ; " But deliver us from evil ;" past, present, and future."

Let us also learn from this prayer, the " Our Father," how pleasing it must be to God to pray for others, for the petitions are all made in common, not for one's self individually. This manner of praying is conformable to the example of our Lord Jesus Christ, and, therefore, it must be most acceptable to Him to remember others in our prayers. Indeed, His whole life was a continual prayer for the just as well as for sinners. " And not for them only (the Apostles) do I pray, but for them also ; who, through their word, shall believe in Me, that they all may be one, as Thou, Father, in me and I in Thee, that they also may be one in Us, that the world may believe that Thou hast sent Me." (John xvii., 20, 21.)

"Pray one for another that you may be saved." (Epis. St. James v. 16:) And we are especially bound to pray for the successor of St. Peter, our Holy Father, the Pope, the Bishops and clergy of the Holy Catholic Church, and for all those who labor for the propagation of our holy faith. This our Lord Jesus Christ exhorts us to do by His example. "And now I am no more in the world; and these (Apostles) are in the world, and I come to Thee. Holy Father, keep them in Thy name, whom Thou hast given Me; that they may be one as We also are. . . . I do not ask that Thou shouldst take them away out of the world, but that Thou shouldst preserve them from evil. Sanctify them in truth. . . . Father, I will that where I am, they also whom Thou hast given Me, may may be with Me; that they may see My glory which Thou hast given Me; (John xvii. 11, 15, 17, 24.) Although we should pray earnestly for the prelates and pastors of the Church, yet we must not forget to recommend to God all poor sinners, as well as infidels, heretics, and schismatics, this is also according to the example of Jesus Christ and the Saints. Our Lord's first prayer, when hanging on the cross, was for the greatest sinners and His most bitter enemies. "Father, forgive them, for they know not what they do." (Luke xxiii. 34.) "He that knoweth his brother to sin a sin which is not unto death, let him ask, and life shall be given to him that sinneth not to death." (I. John v. 16.) St. Ambrose, St. Augustine and the Ven. Bede and others explain the words, "who sinneth not to death," to mean that class of sinners who do not intend to remain obstinate till death, because such would require, says St. Alphonsus, a very extraordinary grace. But for other sinners God promises their conversion if we pray earnestly for them. " Let him ask and life (the life of grace) shall be given him for him that sinneth." The great efficacy of such prayers, when they proceed from the heart, is evinced from a variety of examples. Instances occur every day in which God rescues individuals of every class of sinners from the powers of darkness, and transfers them into the kingdom of His beloved Son, making them from being vessels of wrath, become vessels of mercy, and that in realizing so happy a consummation, the prayers of the pious have considerable influence no one can reasonably doubt, "for God willingly hears the prayer of a Christian," says St. John Chrysostom, " not only when offered for himself, but also for another. Necessity obliges us to pray for ourselves, charity exhorts us to pray for others. The prayer of fraternal charity, he adds, is more acceptable to God than that of necessity." (Chrysost. Hom. 14 oper. imper. in Matt.) The prayer for sinners, says St. Alphonsus, is not only beneficial to them, but is, moreover, most pleasing to God; and the Lord Himself complains of His servants who do not recommend sinners to Him. He said one day to St. Mary Magdalen of Pazzi: "See, my daughter, how the Christians are in the devil's hands, if My elect did not deliver them by their prayers, they would be devoured." Inflamed by these words with holy zeal, this Saint used to offer to God the Blood of the Redeemer fifty times a day in behalf of sinners, and she was quite wasted away with the desire for their conversion. "Ah," she would exclaim, "how great a pain it is, O Lord, to see how one could help Thy creatures by dying for them and not be able to do so." In every one of her spiritual exercises she would recommend sinners to God, and it is related in her life that she scarcely spent an hour in the day without praying for them; she would even frequently arise in the middle of the night to go before the Blessed Sacrament to offer prayers for them. She went so far as to desire to endure even the pains of hell for their conversion, provided she could still love God in that place, and God granted her wish by inflicting on her most violent pains and infirmities for the salvation of sinners; and yet after all this she would shed bitter tears, thinking she did nothing for their conversion. "Ah, Lord, make me die," she would exclaim, "and return to life again as many times as is necessary to satisfy Thy justice for them." God, as is related in her life, did not fail to give the grace of conversion to many sinners on account of her fervent prayers. Hence, St. Alphonsus says: "Souls that really love God will never neglect to pray for poor sinners."

How could it be possible for a person who really loves God and knows His ardent love for our souls, and how much He wishes us to pray for sinners, and how much Jesus Christ has done and suffered for their salvation, how can such a one, I say, look with indifference on so many poor souls, deprived of God's grace, being so many slaves of hell, without feeling moved to importune God with frequent prayers to give light and strength to these wretched beings in order that they may come out of the miserable state of spiritual death in which they are slumbering? True it is, God has not promised to grant our petitions in the case of those who put a positive impediment in the way of their conversion. Yet God, in His Goodness, has often deigned, through the prayers of His servants, to bring back the most blind and obstinate sinners to the way of salvation by means of extraordinary graces. Therefore, we should never fail to recommend poor sinners to God in all our spiritual exercises; moreover, he who prays for others will experience that his prayers for himself will be heard much sooner. In the life of St. Margaret of Cortona, we read that she would pray more than a hundred times a day for the conversion of sinners, and, indeed, so numerous were their conversions, that the Franciscan fathers complained to her of not being able to hear the confessions of all those who were converted by her prayers.

The Curé of Ars, who died a few years since in the odor of sanctity, in one of his catechetical instructions, relates as follows: "A great lady, of one of the first families in France, has been here and went away this morning. She is rich, very rich, and scarcely twenty-three. She has offered herself to God for the conversion of sinners and the expiation of sin. She mortifies herself in a thousand ways, wears a girdle all armed with iron points; her parents know nothing of it; she is as white as a sheet of paper." (Spirit of Curé of Ars.) The same saintly pastor said one day to a priest who complained of not being able to change the hearts of his parishioners for the better, "you prayed, you wept, you sighed, but did you fast also, did you deprive yourself of sleep, did you sleep on the bare ground, did you scourge yourself. Do not think you have done all if you have not yet done these penances." If we do not love poor sinners that much, if we think it above our strength to perform similar penitential works for their conversion, let us at least do something, let us recommend them to the sacred hearts of Jesus and Mary, or offer ourselves for a week or two as a holocaust to

God to be disposed of according to His good pleasure, suffer some cold, some heat, some inconvenience, some contradiction and contempt in silence, let us deny ourselves some agreeable visits, or other natural pleasures; or let us make a Novena, or hear Mass daily for a week and offer up our Communions with this intention. We may be assured by these and such exercises we shall give great pleasure to Jesus Christ, contribute much to the honor of His heavenly Father, win His heart over to ourselves, force it sweetly to give the grace of conversion to many sinners, and obtain for ourselves a large share of Divine Grace.

II.—Our Prayer must be Humble.

"Two men went up into the temple to pray; the one a Pharisee, the other a Publican. The Pharisee, standing, prayed thus to himself: 'O God, I give Thee thanks that I am not as the rest of men, extortioners, unjust adulterers, as also is this Publican. I fast thrice in the week; I give tithes of all I possess.' And the Publican, standing afar off, would not so much as lift up his eyes towards heaven, but struck his breast, saying: 'O Lord, be merciful to me a sinner.' I say to you, this man went down to his house justified rather than the other." (Luke xviii. 10-14.) In this parable of the Pharisee and the Publican, our Lord Jesus

Christ teaches us that prayer without humility obtains nothing. As the Pharisee left the temple just as bad and as sinful as he entered, so shall we not improve by prayer if we pray with the same sentiments of pride and self-conceit. Even common sense tells us that prayer, to be good, must be humble. Should a poor man beg alms in a haughty and impudent manner, he would be despised and rejected by an interior conviction, telling every person that to beg and to be proud at the same time is a most despicable thing; yea, an abomination in the eyes of all men. True beggars know this but too well; they study different manners and ways to show themselves humble; they take the last place; they adopt humble language; if you meet them, they fall prostrate before you, asking alms with joined hands and with tears often artfully expressed. Should they have a good suit of clothes, they will put on ragged and tattered ones when they go out begging. How many humble reasons do they not allege, such as not having eaten anything for the whole day. They pretend they are suffering innumerable infirmities, and so lamentable are their sighs that even hearts of stone could not help feeling for them. No one blames them for this conduct; every one, on the contrary, approves of it, and condemns the opposite manner of acting.

If humility, then, is required from men when asking relief of their fellow-men, how much more

14*

will it not be required from us by the Lord of heaven and earth, when we address Him in prayer? To know that we are sinners, and have so often grievously offended the Divine Majesty ; that we have crucified our Lord Jesus Christ by our heinous sins ; to know that if God did not assist us every day we would commit most shameful and atrocious crimes, becoming even worse than the brute, is undoubtedly a sufficient reason why we should always remain humble, and pray with sentiments of exterior and interior humility, saying with the Publican, " Lord be merciful to me a sinner," that we, like him, may always come forth from prayer more acceptable, more justified, and more sanctified in the sight of God, the Lord of heaven and earth. " From the beginning have the proud not been acceptable to Thee," said Judith, " but the prayer of the humble and the meek hath always pleased Thee." (Judith ix., 16.)

How great was not the wisdom which Solomon, the Wise, received in prayer. But in what manner and, with what sentiments did he pray? Holy Writ says that Solomon, when praying, " had fixed both knees on the ground, and had spread his hands towards heaven." (III. Kings, viii., 54.) St. Stephen effected by his prayer the conversion of St. Paul the Apostle, and many others of his enemies. But how humble was not his prayer. " Falling on his knees," says Holy Scripture, " he cried with a loud voice, saying: Lord, lay not this sin to their charge." (Acts vii., 59.) How humble must not have been the prayer of St. James the Apostle; for most of the time he would pray on his knees; for this reason the skin of his knees had become as hard as that of a camel. St. John Chrysostom adds that also the skin of his forehead had become quite hard from lying with it prostrate on the ground whilst at prayer. Ribadeneira and others relate the same of St. Bartholomew the Apostle.

The good thief received the forgiveness of his sins, but before asking it, he humbled himself, avowing before the whole world what he was, and what he had deserved. "We receive the due reward of our deeds." (Luke xxiii., 41.) The woman of Canaan suffers herself to be compared to a dog by our Lord Jesus Christ; she does not feel herself insulted by this comparison, believing, as she did, that she deserved this name. Our dear Saviour wondered at this, saying: "Oh, woman, great is thy faith." (Math. xv., 28.) Her faith was so great because her humility was astonishingly great. Hence she heard from the mouth of our Lord these consoling words: "Be it done to thee as thou wilt." The prodigal son says: "Father, I have sinned against heaven and before thee; I am not now worthy to be called thy son; make me as one of thy hired servants." (Luke xv., 18.) The father, seeing this great humility and sorrow in his son, forgot all his guilt at once, receiving him as one of his best children. God will treat us in the same manner, if we present ourselves before Him with the like sentiments of humility and unworthiness. When our Lord Jesus Christ said to the Centurion, "I will come and heal thy servant," the Centurion answered: "Lord, I am not worthy that Thou should enter under my roof." (Math. viii., 8.) This humility and faith of the Centurion pleased our Saviour so much that He said to him: "Go, and as thou hast believed, so be it done to thee, and the servant was healed at the same hour." (Math. viii., 13.)

Now, in what manner did our Lord Jesus Christ Himself pray. "Kneeling down, he prayed." (Luke xxii., 47.) Nay, He did more: "He fell upon His face praying and saying: 'My Father, if it be possible, let this chalice pass from me.'" (Math. xxvi., 39.) St. Thais did not even dare so much as to pronounce the name of God when praying, after her conversion from her sinful life. Hence she would say: "Thou Who madest me have pity on me." St. Paul the hermit, was so much accustomed to pray on his knees, and with his hands lifted up to heaven, that he died in this posture, remaining so after death. Is it, then, astonishing that the Saints should have received so many and so great favors from God, since their humility was so great and so pleasing to Him? "To the humble God giveth grace," says the Apostle St. James. "Their prayer shall pierce the clouds." (Eccles. xxxv., 21.)

"Yes," says St. Alphonsus, "should a soul have committed ever so many sins, yet the Lord will not reject it, if it knows how to humble itself." "A contrite and humble heart, O God, Thou wilt not despise." (Ps. l. 19). As He is severe and inexorable to the proud, so is He bountiful, merciful and liberal to the humble. "Know, My daughter," said Jesus Christ one day to St. Catherine of Sienna, "that whosoever shall humbly persevere in asking graces of Me, shall obtain all virtues." "Never did I," said St. Teresa, "receive more favors from the Lord, than when I humbled myself before His divine Majesty."

III.—Our Prayer must be Fervent.

Well hath Isaias prophesied of you saying, "this people honoreth me with their lips; but their heart is far from me." (Matt. xv. 8.) In these words our Saviour gives us to understand, that a prayer which proceeds not from the heart, or which is not devout and fervent, is not heard by His Heavenly Father. There are many Christians who recite their prayers without thinking of what they say. Should they be required to tell what they asked of our Lord, they would be at a loss for an answer. The prayers of such Christians are quite powerless with God. As the pipes of an organ will not produce their musical sounds unless inflated by the bellows, so, in the same manner, prayer, unless prompted by the fervor of the heart, will fail to be agreeable to the ears of God. One Our Father, said with fervor, is better and obtains more from God than the entire Rosary recited a dozen times in a careless manner. St. Bernard once saw how an angel of the Lord wrote down in a book the divine praises of each of his brethren when they were reciting the Divine Office; some were written in letters of gold to express the devotion and fervor with which they were recited; others in letters of silver, on account of the pure intention with which they were performed; others were written with ink, to signify that they were said by way of routine and in a slothful manner; others again were written with water color, to indicate that they had been performed with great lukewarmness and without devotion or fervor. Of some religious the divine praises were not written down at all, but instead of the chanted psalms, the following words were written: "This people honoreth Me with their lips, but their heart is far from Me," (Isai. xxix. 13.) to signify that the Angel of the Lord was much displeased with this kind of prayer.

Holy Angels! show us once your book that we

may see in what colors the prayers of so many Christians are written down, especially in time of prosperity, when no calamity forces them to have recourse to God. There is good reason to fear, that the prayers of many are written down in letters of ink, others in water color, and the greater number of them, I fear, are not written down at all; so that the devil himself must rejoice and laugh at them, as he did at the prayers of two friars, of whom Jourdanus speaks: "They recited the Divine Office in such a careless manner, that at the conclusion of it, the devil appeared and cast an intolerable odor around, at the same time, exclaiming with great laughter, such incense is due to such prayer." Moreover, how many are there not who say their prayers without being at all in earnest to obtain what they ask. They recite, for instance, the Our Father a hundred, yea, a thousand times, without wishing, at all, that any of its seven petitions should be granted. Let us examine them briefly. The first petition is: "Hallowed be Thy name," that is, give me, and to all men, the grace to know Thee always better and better; to honor, praise, glorify, and love Thee; to comprehend the greatness of Thy blessings, the duration of Thy promises, the sublimity of Thy Majesty, and the depth of Thy judgments. All this is included in the first petition of the Our Father. But where are those who truly and sincerely wish this for themselves and for others. This is not wished for by any of those who, when entering the church, do not even think of bending the knee to express their faith in the name of God.

Secondly, nor by those who do not desire to listen to the divine word in sermons and Christian instructions, that they may better learn their duty towards God, themselves and their fellow-men.

Thirdly, nor by those who never think of praying fervently for the conversion of sinners, heretics, Jews, or heathens.

Fourthly, nor by those who dishonor the name of God, by cursing and swearing, thus teaching others the language of the devil.

Fifthly, nor by those who are ashamed of giving good example, who think, speak and act bad, when others do the same.

Sixthly, nor by all those who grievously transgress any of the Commandments of God, and thus dishonor, despise and insult the name of God. Such as these, certainly, do not praise and honor God's name, and yet with their lips they will always pray: "Hallowed be Thy name," without contributing anything at all towards the glory of the Lord of heaven and earth. Of these we must think, that they know not what they ask or do, nor wish to obtain what they ask.

The second petition is, "Thy kingdom come." Where are those who truly wish that God alone should reign in their hearts, and that no creature might have any part in it? Alas! most men feel provoked at the least temporal loss, at the slightest harsh word. And what account do the generality of men make of the grace and friendship of God? The readiness with which they commit sin, tells it sufficiently. How difficult is it not for the priest to prevail upon them so far as to make them go to confession and Holy Communion? How seldom do they pray? Shall we then believe that those who neglect and refuse the means to acquire the grace of God do earnestly pray, "Thy kingdom come?" And where are they who truly desire to leave this world for a better one? Alas! should death knock at their door, what mourning, what alarm, what tears would it produce. Nay, many even are so much attached to this life, that should God offer them the choice between heaven and earth, they would prefer the latter; let them pray, sigh and exclaim: "Thy kingdom come," their prayer is not true, because they do not wish for God's Kingdom. And where are those who are in earnest when they pray: "Thy will be done on earth as it is in heaven." Were God to say to them: "Well, it is My will that you should undergo humiliations and contempt; and for this end I will make use of your neighbor, of your friend, of your companion. Like Job, you shall endure the loss of your good name and your honor among your fellow-men, or of your children and all your earthly goods," how soon would every one of them change his prayer; Lord, be it otherwise done to me, as I do not mean this when I pray: "Thy will be done on earth as it is in heaven."

The fourth petition is: "Give us this day our daily bread." That is, give us everything necessary for the support of our temporal and spiritual life. Of course, no one refuses the temporal; but where are those who truly hunger and thirst after the food of their souls; after prayer, the Word of God, Confession and Holy Communion? This food is relished by the smallest number of men only, which is an evident proof that they do not wish to be heard when they make this petition.

"And forgive us our trespasses as we forgive them that have trespassed against us." Neither does this fifth petition of our Father proceed from the heart of most of men. They all, of course, wish that God should forgive them every sin, guilt and punishment, but they themselves do not want to forgive. How long do they not preserve, in their hearts, a certain aversion, rancor, even enmity, caused by a little harsh word, insult or detraction of their fellow-men? To greet them, to speak to or pray for them, seems too hard; against such persons they must speak uncharitably; slander them on every favorable opportunity; nay, even curse them. How can they be sincere in saying:

"Forgive us our trespasses as we forgive them that have trespassed against us?" They ask forgiveness of God in the same way as they forgive others. Certainly, their prayer is untrue, therefore, they are insincere in this manner of praying.

"Lead us not into temptation"—that is, Lord, preserve us from the temptations of the devil, of the flesh, and of the world. But alas! most men love the occasion of temptations, and betake themselves wilfully unto them. How should the Lord, then, preserve them from temptations? Most assuredly they do not wish at all to be heard in making this petition.

"And deliver us from evil"—that is, preserve us from sin; but the greater number of men commit them deliberately every day, not doing the least violence to themselves by trying to avoid the occasions thereof; or to have immediate recourse to prayer in the moment of temptation; or to receive the Sacraments frequently. As they do not make use of the means which God has given us to be preserved from sin, how can they pray in truth or in earnest: "Deliver us from evil?" They do not mean it. In conclusion, to all these petitions they say: "Amen"—that is, Lord, grant everything that we have asked in these seven petitions. But as often as these petitions are repeated by most men, as often do they prove untrue; and the word *Amen* is also identified in the same untruthfulness:

"We do not mean or desire it in this sense." What, then, must Almighty God think of such a prayer? What would you think of me were I to ask of you what you knew I would be afraid to receive? Would you not consider me as a rash man, wanting to test your kindness and liberality, or to turn it into ridicule? Certainly, you would feel angry, and order me away from your presence. Will the Lord, then, who knows full well what is meant in my prayer, hear me, although my conscience tells me that I do not sincerely wish to be heard? Will He force His gifts and graces upon us whilst we do not appreciate them, or have any real desire for them; nay, are even afraid of receiving them? Will He hear such a prayer?

We must, then, be in earnest to obtain by our prayer what we ask in it. "Wilt thou be made whole?" said our Lord to the man languishing thirty-eight years. (John v. 6.) "What will ye that I do to you?" our Lord asked the two blind men. (Matt. xxix. 32.) Had He noticed that they were not in earnest in their petition for health, He would have left them alone. Holy Scripture says of those who pray to God in earnest and with fervor, that they *cry* to the Lord. Thus holy David says of himself: "In my trouble I cried to the Lord and He heard me." (Ps. cxix. 1.) And the Lord has promised to hear such a prayer. "He shall cry to Me and I will hear him." (Ps. lxl.

15.) Now, to cry to the Lord means, according to St. Bernard, to pray with an earnest and great desire to be heard. The greater this desire is the more piercing is this cry of prayer to the ears of God. In vain do we hope that God will hear our prayer if it be destitute of this earnest desire, fervor, sighing, crying and effusion of the heart. Hence the prophet Jeremias says: "Arise, give praise in the night, in the beginning of the watches; pour out thy heart like water before the face of the Lord; lift up thy hands to Him for the life of thy little children that have fainted for hunger." (Jeremias ii. 19.) Now, what is it to pour out our heart before the Lord? It is to pray, to sigh, to cry with a most vehement desire to be heard by our Lord. Hence St. Bernard says: "Great crying in the ears of the Lord is a vehement desire," for God considers more the ardent desire and love of the heart than the cries of the lips. And St. Paul says, in his Epistle to the Romans: "The spirit himself asketh for us with unspeakable groanings." (Ch. viii. 26.) Hence the royal prophet says of his prayer: "In His sight I pour out my prayer." (Ps. cxli. 3.) And in Ps. (lxi. 9.) he says: "Pour out your heart before Him." It was thus that Anna poured out her heart before the Lord and obtained the holy child Samuel. (I Kings i. 15.) "As Anna had her heart full of grief, she prayed to the Lord, shedding many tears; and it came to

15*

pass, as she multiplied prayers before the Lord," etc. ; here the holy Fathers ask what is meant by this long prayer of Anna, since she besought the Lord only in a few words to grant her a child. St. John Chrysostom answers and says: "Although her prayer consisted of a few words, yet it was long, on account of the interior fervor and ardent desire with which she poured out her heart before the Lord, for she prayed more with her heart than with her lips, according to what is related in Holy Scripture: "Now Anna spoke from her heart, whilst her lips only moved, but her voice was silent." (I Kings i. 13.) "Our Lord will, therefore, hear us, provided we understand how to pour out our hearts in prayer—that is, to lay open before Him all the wishes and desires of our soul, its griefs, sufferings, cares, solicitudes and anxieties, laying them, as it were, into His paternal heart and into the bosom of His Divine Providence, in order that He may come to aid, relieve and comfort us." Nay, according to St. Paul, we ought to do still more. In his Epistle to the Ephesians, (chap. vi. 18.) we read: "By all prayer and supplication, praying at all times in the spirit," he wishes us to understand that we ought to go as far as even to conjure God by everything sacred, beseeching Him, by the death of our Divine Saviour upon the cross, and by the precious blood of Jesus Christ; by sighing, crying, and striking our breast; by falling prostrate and

QUALITIES OF PRAYER. 171

the like, in order to manifest the most earnest fervor and ardent desire of our heart in prayer. Should we, then, experience, in our will, a certain languor, sloth and tepidity; nay, even a certain repugnance and resistance to ask favors of God with fervor and earnestness, we must beseech our dear Lord, as the Holy Church does in one of her prayers, to compel our rebellious wills, by means best calculated to effect this holy fervor in our hearts, in order that we may make sure of being heard and of receiving what we pray for.

In order to produce this holy fervor in our hearts, God often sends us troubles, crosses, sickness, and adversities of every description, nothing being better calculated to make us pray with fervor than afflictions, tribulations and crosses. Let the soul be under heavy sufferings which it would like to cast off, surely it will not need a prayer-book. Then, like unto hungry beggars, it finds a flow of words to produce the most heartfelt and fervent prayer. In prosperous times the prayer-book is recurred to, but in the hour of adversity it is the heart that speaks. If before the lips only moved, it is now the whole heart that is put in motion, from its over-great desire to be heard and find relief and comfort. Then, like David, men will say: "All the day I cried to Thee, O Lord. I stretched out my hands to Thee." (Ps. lxxxvii., 10.) "Consider and hear me, O Lord, my God." (Ps. xii., 4.)

Such prayers are most pleasing to God, and He cannot refuse hearing them, according to what David says : " In my trouble I cried to the Lord, and he heard me." (Ps. cxix., 1.) Holy Scripture abounds in examples of this truth. When the Prophet Jonas was swallowed by the whale, and carried about in the depths of the ocean, he prayed most fervently to the Lord, his God, saying : " Thou hast cast me forth into the heart of the deep sea, and a flood hath encompassed me ; all Thy billows and waves have passed over me." (Jonas ii., 4.) He then said, "I cried out in my affliction to the Lord, and *He heard me*. I cried out of the belly of hell, and *Thou hast heard my voice.*" (Verse 3.) How great was the affliction of Sara, on being accused of having murdered seven husbands, but who were killed by a devil named Asmodeus at their first going in unto her. At this reproach, says Holy Scripture, she went into an upper chamber of her house, and for three days and three nights did neither eat nor drink, but continuing in prayer with tears, besought God to deliver her from this reproach. " And her prayers were heard in the sight of the glory of the Most High God." (Job iii., 10, 11.) With what great fervor did not the Apostles cry out to our Lord Jesus Christ amidst the storms of the sea. " Lord save us, we perish." And He heard their cry, and commanded the winds and the sea, and there came a great calm. (Math.

viii., 25, 26.) Yes, in tribulation is truly verified what is related by the Ruler in the Gospel: "And he himself believed and his whole house." (John iv., 53.) Not only one member of the family will pray; nay, father, mother, children, servants, relatives, will unite in beseeching the Lord for assistance, because grief and affliction have come upon the whole house. Thus the Latin proverb is verified: "Qui nescit orare, eat ad mare." Let him who does not know how to pray with fervor make a voyage at sea. There the storms and dangers of death will teach him to pour forth most fervent prayers. Such prayers are most powerful with and heard by the Lord.

I cannot omit remarking that tears in prayer are most powerful with God to obtain our petitions. The Fathers of the Church are profuse in bestowing praises upon humble tears of the soul. The Holy Scriptures and the lives of the Saints abound in examples to prove their power with God. "O, how great is the power which the tears of sinners exercise with God," says St. Peter Chrysologus. (Serm. 93.) "They water heaven, wash the earth clean, deliver from hell, and prevail upon God to recall the sentence of damnation pronounced over every mortal sin." "Yes," says Anselmus Laudunensis, commenting on the words of the Book of Tobias, chap. iii., 11, "continuing in prayer, with tears he besought God." "Prayer appeases God, but if tears are added, He feels overcome and unable to resist any longer. The former is for him an odoriferous balm—the latter is a sweet tyranny." Hence Julianus (lib. de. Ligno Vitæ, c. ix.) exclaims with truth : " O, humble tears, how great is your power, how great is your reign ! You need not fear the Tribunal of the Eternal Judge; you silence all your accusers, and no one dares to prevent you from approaching the Lord ; should you enter alone you will not come out empty. What more ! You conquer the unconquerable, you bind the Omnipotent, you open heaven, you chase all the devils." "Indeed," says Peter Cellensis, (lib. de Panibus, c. xii.,) "the infernal spirits find the flames of hell more supportable than our tears." Hence Cornelius a Lapide remarks : "One tear of the sinner, produced by the sorrow of his heart, is capable of making God forgive and forget many, even the most atrocious crimes." For this reason, St. Leo the Pope, says of the tears of St. Peter, (Serm. 9 de passione) : "O ! happy tears of thine, O holy Apostle St. Peter, which were for thee a holy baptism to cancel thy sin of denying the Lord." St. Magdalen asks of our Lord the forgiveness of her numerous and great sins; but in what manner? "She began to wash His sacred feet with her tears." (Luke vii. 38), and these tears moved His compassionate heart, by saying, "Many sins are forgiven her, because she hath loved much." Why was it that the holy patriarch Jacob, when wrestling with the angel of the Lord, received his blessing? (Gen. xxxii.) it was because he asked it with tears in his eyes. "He wept and made supplication to him." (Osee xii. 4.) In the fourth Book of Kings, chap. xx., we read as follows: "In these days Ezechias was sick unto death, and Isaias the prophet came to him and said: Thus saith the Lord God: give charge concerning thy house, for thou shalt die and not live. And he turned his face to the wall and prayed to the Lord saying: I beseech Thee, O Lord, remember how I have walked before Thee in truth, and with a perfect heart, and have done that which is pleasing before Thee. And Ezechias *wept with much weeping.*" What was the effect of it? Hearken: "And before Isaias was gone out of the middle of the court, the word of the Lord came to him saying: Go back and tell Ezechias, thus saith the Lord: I have heard thy prayer and I have seen thy tears; and behold I have healed thee; on the third day thou shalt go up to the Temple of the Lord. And I will add to thy days fifteen years." Our Lord Jesus Christ Himself often prayed with tears in His eyes, according to what St. Paul the Apostle writes: "Who in the days of His flesh, *with a strong cry and tears offering up prayers and supplication, was heard* for His reverence." (Heb. v. 7.) In his comment, chap. xii. of Zacharee, Cornelius a Lapide relates that St.

Dunstan, after the death of King Edwin, from whom he had received many ill treatments, saw, whilst at prayer, several black men running off with the soul of the king in their hands. Forgetting all the injuries and ill treatments which he had received from Edwin, he took pity on him in his miserable condition, shedding torrents of tears before the face of the Lord, for the deliverance of the king's soul, and he did not cease weeping and praying until the Lord heard him. Soon after, he saw the same black men again, but their hands were empty, and the soul of the king was no longer in their possession. They then commenced to curse, and swear, and utter the most abominable imprecations against the servant of God, to which St. Dunstan paid no attention, but thanked God for the extraordinary great mercy shown to the king." Let us, then, with Judith (chap. viii. 14), pray to the Lord with tears, asking His pardon, His graces, and all His favors, and let us rest assured, that as a mother cannot help consoling her weeping child, neither will our dear Lord refuse the petitions of our weeping souls.

IV.—Our Prayer must be Followed by Amendment of Life.

The sinner who prays to God for salvation without having the desire to quit the state of sin, must not expect to be heard. "There are," says St. Alphonsus, "some unhappy persons, who love the chains with which the devil keeps them bound like slaves. The prayers of such are never heard by God; because they are rash, presumptuous and abominable. For what greater presumption can there be than for a man to ask favors of a Prince, whom he not only has often offended, but whom he intends to offend again?" And this is the meaning of the words of the Holy Spirit, when He says, that the prayer of him who turns away his ears so as not to hear what God commands, is detestable and odious to God: "He who turneth away his ears from learning the law, his prayer shall be an abomination." (Prov. xxviii. 9.) To these people God says, "it is of no use your praying to Me, for I will turn My eyes from you and will not hear you: when you stretch forth your hands I will turn away My eyes from you, and when you multiply prayer I will not hear." (Isai. i. 15.) Why was the Lord so severe to the Jews, His chosen people, inflicting upon them the hardest punishments, such as the Egyptian bondage in which they suffered for so many years? How often did they not pray for their deliverance? And why did the Lord not hear them? The prophet Ezechiel says: "And they committed fornication in Egypt; in their youth they committed fornication." (Chap. xxiii. 3.) Hence they prayed and cried to God in vain. But, no sooner had they done away with their sins of idolatry and fornication, than the Lord graciously heard them. "And the children of Israel, groaning, cried out, because of the works; and their cry went up unto God from the works, and He heard their groaning, and remembered the covenant which He made with Abraham, Isaac and Jacob; and the Lord looked upon the children of Israel, and He knew them." (Enoch. ii. 23, 25.) The Ark of the Covenant was a great treasure for the Jews. When it was carried around the city of Jerico, the walls of the city fell down; when the Jews had arrived with it at the river Jordan, the waters of the river divided, the lower part flowing off and the upper part rising like a mountain. Now, after the Jews had lost four thousand men in one day, in a war against the Philistines, they had the Ark brought into the camp, hoping by this that the Lord would protect them, and deliver their enemies into their hands." And the ancients of Israel said: " Why hath the Lord defeated us to-day before the Philistines? Let us fetch unto us the Ark of the Covenant of the Lord from Silo, and let it come in the midst of us that it may save us from the hands of our enemies. And when the Ark of the Covenant of the Lord was come into the camp, all Israel shouted with a great joy, and the earth rang again." (I. Kings iv.) Now, they thought they had no more to fear from other enemies, who, at the sight of the Ark of the Covenant, were panic-stricken, so much so, that they cried out: "God is come into the camp." And sighing they said: "Woe to us; who shall deliver us from the hands of these high Gods?" With new courage they commenced to fight. Were they victorious? By no means; they were defeated worse than ever, losing thirty thousand men, besides the Ark of the Covenant. One might ask here: Did God then cease to love the Israelites? Most assuredly not, His love still remained the same as before. Why, then, were they defeated in the presence of the Ark of the Covenant, which was given to them as a sign of the divine blessing and protection? "But for the love of His Ark," says Theodoret, "God did not wish to protect His people, because, after having grievously offended Him, they did not repent of their sins. It was with sinful hearts they paid outward honor to the Ark. They shouted with great joy as soon as they beheld it, but there was not one who shed a tear of repentance, no one prayed and sighed with a sorrowful heart. Hence, the Ark brought down no blessing upon them at that period." " Why, then, should we wonder," says Dionysius, the Carthusian, "if we see miseries and calamities increase among the Christians, notwithstanding their prayer to avert them. 'Tis because they pray with sinful and criminal hearts, not being sorry, in the least, for their evil deeds, nor showing the slightest desire to amend their lives." Let them wear upon their persons as many Agnus Deis, Relics of the Saints, Gospels of St. John as they may wish; let them even pray and cry to heaven as much as they will, all these articles of devotion, prayers and cries will be of no avail, if, at the same time, they rent out their hearts to the devil, not wishing to give up his worship and service. Instead of being heard, they will, according to St. Augustine, be so much the more severely punished. "Punishments," says the Saint, "become more frequent every day, because the number of sins is daily increasing."

If, therefore, we wish God to hear our prayers, we must endeavor to be sorry for our sins and amend our lives. "Above all," says St. Ambrose, "we must weep and then pray." The Lord Himself has declared this quite distinctly by the prophet Isaias: "I will not hear you;" why not? "for your hands are full of blood;" (Isaias i. 15,) full of sins and iniquities.

But, on the contrary, the Lord has promised, by the same prophet, that He will hear the prayers of those who truly amend their lives. "Loose the bands of wickedness; undo the bundles that oppress. .... Then shalt thou call, and the Lord shall hear; thou shalt cry, and He shall say: Here I am," (Isai. lviii.), that is to help you. By the command of God, the Prophet Jonas had to announce to the Ninivites that within forty days their city would be destroyed. The Ninivites at once commenced to pray to God and ask His pardon. God heard their prayers. Why? Because they repented of their sins, did penance for them and amended their lives. The prayers of a true and sincere repentant, are acceptable in the sight of God and heard by Him. Hence, according to the advice of St. Paul, we must endeavor always to pray to God with a contrite heart. "I will, therefore, that men pray in every place, lifting up pure hands." (I. Tim. ii. 8.) When are our hearts pure? "If they are free of sin," says St. Ambrose.

From what has been said, the sinner should, however, not infer that, being a sinner and in the disgrace of God, his prayer could not be acceptable to God, and therefore abandon it. No, it would be entirely wrong for a sinner to argue thus. For as long as he does not sin unto death, that is, if he has not the will to live and die in sin, but desires to amend his life, and prays for it, God will listen to his prayer, and hear it, if he perseveres in it. "There are others," says St. Alphonsus, "who sin through frailty, or by the violence of some great passion, and who groan under the yoke of the enemy, and who desire to break these chains of death and to escape from their miserable slavery, let them ask the assistance of God; for their prayer, if persevered in, will certainly be heard, for Jesus Christ has said: "Every one that asks receives, and he who seeks grace finds it." (Math. vii. 8.) His prayer, it is true, is not heard on account of his meritorious works, which he does not possess, but is heard through the merits and promises of Jesus Christ, Who has declared to hear every one that asks. "Therefore, when we pray," says St. Thomas, "it is not necessary to be friends of God, in order to obtain the grace we ask; for prayer itself restores His friendship to us." Hence, St. Bernard says: "The desire of the sinner to escape from sin is a gift which is certainly given by no other than God Himself, Who most undoubtedly would not give this holy desire to the sinner unless He intended to hear him." Witness the publican in the Gospel, who went into the temple to pray: "And the publican standing afar off would not so much as lift up his eyes towards heaven; but struck his breast, saying: O God, be merciful to me a sinner. I say to you, this man went down into his house justified." (Luke viii. 13–14.)

But the sinner may say, I have no sorrow for my sins, and do not desire to amend my life, therefore, according to what you have said, God will not hear my prayer, consequently I may abandon it altogether. I answer, by no means relinquish it; you must not, on this account, give up your prayer, although God will not hear you as long as you persevere in these dispositions of heart; yet, for the sake of your prayer, God spares you, waiting patiently for your conversion. "Hence no sinner," says St. Alphonsus, "should ever give up his prayer, as otherwise he would be lost forever. God would sooner send sinners to hell, if they ceased to pray, yet, on account of their perseverance in prayer, He still spares them." But let him who has no sorrow for his sins, no desire for the amendment of his life, ask of God this sorrow and grace of a thorough conversion, and let him persevere in asking for it, if he does, he may rest assured that God will finally enlighten his mind by making him understand the miserable state in which he is living, and touch his heart with sorrow for it, and also strengthen his will to make serious efforts to rise from it. Another will say, I have not only no sorrow for my sins, but I have not even the least desire to ask God's grace to be sorry for them. How can I, then, pray, not having the least desire to obtain anything? This, I must confess, is a pitiable but not a desperate state, for, if you will pray with perseverance, God will give you the desire to pray for the grace of contrition. Has He not declared: "I desire not the death of the wicked, but that he be converted and live?" God has the greatest desire to see all sinners saved, and is ready at any time to give them the graces necessary for their salvation; but He wishes that they should pray for every good thought and desire, and for efficacious grace to put their good desires into execution. Let such a sinner pray: " Lord, give me a true desire to pray to Thee for my salvation;" let him persevere in thus praying, and then let him rest assured that he will not be lost. The conversion of King Manasses is a most striking proof of this truth. Manasses was twelve years old when his father died. He succeeded him on the throne, but not in his piety and fear of the Lord. As pious as the father was, so impious was the son towards God and His people. He introduced again all the abominations of the Gentiles which the Lord had extirpated from among the children of Israel; he apostatized from the Lord; he introduced again and encouraged idolatry; even in the temple of the Lord he erected an altar to Baal; he introduced into the temple of the true God such abominations as were never heard of before, and which are too shameful to relate. To crown his impiety, he made his son pass through fire in honor of Moloch; used divination, observed omens, appointed pythons and multiplied soothsayers to do evil before the Lord and to provoke Him. (IV Kings, xxi. 1-7.) The Lord often warned him by His prophets, but in vain. At last "the Lord spoke to His prophets, saying: Because Manasses, king of Juda, hath done these most wicked abominations, beyond all that the Amorrhites did before him, and hath made Juda also to sin with his filthy doings, therefore, thus saith the Lord the God of Israel: Behold, I will bring on evils upon Jerusalem and Juda, that whosoever shall hear of them both his ears shall tingle. I will stretch over Jerusalem the line of Samaria and the weight of the house of Achab, and I will efface Jerusalem, as tables are wont to be effaced . . . and I will deliver them into the hands of their enemies, and they shall become a prey and a spoil to all their enemies." (Vers. 10.-14.) Manasses, instead of entering into himself, added cruelty to idolatry. He shed so much innocent blood that, to use the words of Holy Writ, "he filled Jerusalem up to the mouth." (Verse 16.) According to Josephus (Antt. x. 31), "he went, in his contempt for God, so far as to kill all the just of the children of Israel, not sparing even the prophets, but taking away their lives day by day, so that streams of blood were flowing through the streets of Jerusalem." Now, do you think such an impious wretch could be converted? Oh, wonderful power of prayer! So great is thy efficacy with God, that a man, should he be ever so impious and perverse, will not fail to obtain forgiveness of God if he prays for it with a sincere heart. "And the

Lord," says Holy Writ, " brought upon Jerusalem the captains of the army of the king of the Assyrians, and they took Manasses and carried him, bound with chains and fetters, to Babylon. In this great distress and affliction, he entered into himself, and he prayed to the Lord his God and did penance exceedingly before the God of his fathers, and he entreated Him and he besought Him earnestly; and the Lord heard his prayer and brought him again to Jerusalem unto his kingdom. From that time forward he endeavored to serve the Lord the more fervently the more grievously he had offended Him. He abolished idolatry, destroyed the temples, altars, groves on the high places put up in honor of heathenish deities ; repaired the altar of Jehova, in the temple of Jerusalem, and sacrificed upon it victims and peace offerings and offerings of praise, and he commanded Juda to serve the Lord the God of Israel." (II Paral. 33.)

I again repeat what I have said elsewhere: How great will be the pain and misery of the damned, seeing that they might have been saved so easily, provided they had prayed to God for their salvation. How true is it not what St. Alphonsus says: " All spiritual writers in their books, all preachers in their sermons, all confessors in their instructions to their penitents should not inculcate anything more strongly than continual prayer ; they should always admonish, exclaim, and continually repeat:

pray, pray, never cease to pray, for if you pray your salvation will be secure; but if you leave off praying your damnation will be certain. All preachers and directors ought to do this, because, according to the opinion of every Catholic school, there is no doubt of this truth that he who prays obtains grace and is saved ; but those who practise it are too few, and this is why so few are saved." (Chap. iv. on Prayer.)

V.—OUR PRAYER MUST BE UNITED WITH FORGIVENESS OF INJURIES.

" And when you shall stand to pray, forgive if you have aught against any man." (Mark xi. 25.) " Leave thy offering before the Altar, and go first to be reconciled to thy brother, and then coming thou shalt offer thy gift." (Matt. v. 23.)

In these words our Lord Jesus Christ teaches us that our prayer will not please His heavenly Father, nor be heard by Him so long as we entertain in our hearts feelings of dislike towards any of our fellow-men. If you have recourse to prayer, He says, and at the same time have aught against any man, go first and be reconciled to your brother, or at least forgive him from the bottom of your heart, and then come and offer up your prayers, otherwise I will not even listen to you. He has made every man his representative on earth by creating him according to His own image and likeness; He has redeemed all men with His most precious Blood; He has, therefore declared that whatever we do to the least of our fellow-men for His sake we do to Him. Now, by commanding us to love our enemies, to do good to those that hate us, and to pray for those that persecute and calumniate us, (Matt. v. 44.) He asks of us to give to Him in the person of His representatives that which we can give so easily. It would be great presumption to ask His gifts and favors without being willing on our part, to give Him what He requires of us in all justice. To refuse this request of our Lord would, indeed, on our part, be great injustice. We ask of Him the greatest gifts, such as the pardon of innumerable and most grievous offences, final perseverance, deliverance from hell, everlasting glory, and so many other countless favors for both body and soul. What He asks of us is little or nothing compared with His graces.

I will give you what I can, says He, if you give Me what you can. If you will not, neither am I bound to give anything to you. Hence, I have said, " that if two of you shall consent upon earth concerning anything whatsoever they shall ask, it shall be done to them by my Father, Who is in heaven." (Matt. xviii. 19.) Our Saviour means here to say that your heavenly Father is so much pleased with the prayers of those who have no feelings of hatred towards one another, that He will grant to them whatsoever they ask of Him ; but if, on the contrary, they entertain such feelings, their prayer will not be heard. "As singing is not pleasing nor attractive to any one if the voices are not in perfect harmony, so neither," says Origen, "will the prayers of Christian congregations give any pleasure to God if they be not of one heart and one soul, nor will He hear their prayer."

We must, then, whenever we betake ourselves to prayer, banish from our hearts all willful enmity, hatred, rancor, and all uncharitable sentiments which may arise in our soul, by saying a short but fervent prayer for all those towards whom such feelings arise, or by offering up to God for each one of them the precious Blood of Jesus Christ, and all His merits, in union with those of His blessed Mother, and of all His Saints.

To pray for those who wish us evil is an extremely difficult act, and one of the most heroic charity. It is an act free of self-love and self-interest, which is not only counselled but even commanded by our Lord. (Matt. v. 44.) The insults, calumnies, and persecutions of our enemies, relate directly to our own person, wherefore, if we forgive, nay, even beg God also to forgive our enemies, we give up our claim to our right and honor, thus raising ourselves to the great dignity of true children of God, nay even to an unspeakably sublime resemblance to His divinity, according to what Jesus Christ says: "If you pray for those who hate, calumniate and persecute you, you will be children of your Father, Who is in heaven, Who maketh His sun to rise upon the good and bad, and raineth upon the just and the unjust;" (Matt. v. 45,) to whom there is nothing more peculiar, nothing more honorable than to have mercy and to spare; to do good to all his enemies, converting them to be His friends, His children and heirs of His everlasting glory.

Now, by imitating His goodness in a point most averse to our nature, we give Him the greatest glory, and do such violence to His tender and meek Heart as to cause it not only to forgive the sin of our enemies, but even to force it to grant all our prayers. He does so because He wishes to be far more indulgent, far more merciful, and far more liberal than it is possible for us ever to be. Holy Scripture, and the lives of the Saints, furnish us with most striking examples in proof of this great and most consoling truth.

The greatest persecutor of St. Stephen was St. Paul the Apostle before his conversion, for, according to St. Augustine, he threw stones at him by the hands of all those whose clothes he was guarding. What made him from being a persecutor of the Church, become her greatest Apostle and Doctor?

do His will perfectly, that He not only grants their prayers, but even anticipates them. Tauler relates (serm. 1, de Circumcis.) of a pious virgin, whose spiritual director he was, that many people would come and recommend their affairs to her prayers. She always promised to pray for them, but would often forget to do so. Nevertheless, the wishes of those who had recommended themselves to her prayers would be fulfilled. Now, these persons would come and thank her, feeling persuaded that through her prayers God had helped them. She would blush and confess that although she had intended to pray for them, she had forgotten to do so. Wishing to know the reason why our Lord blessed all those who recommended themselves to her prayers, she said to Him: "Why, O Lord, dost Thou bless all those who recommend themselves to my prayers, notwithstanding my forgetfulness to recommend them?" Our Lord answered her, "My daughter, from that very day on which you gave up your will, in order always to do Mine, I gave up Mine to do yours, wherefore I even comply with the pious intentions which you forget to carry out."

Thus it is true what the Lord has promised by the Prophet Isaias, (chap. lxv. 24.) "And it shall come to pass that before they call I will hear." Would to God that all men could understand what has just been said, and practise it most faithfully. How happy would they make themselves and others. Let us often say the following prayer of the Church, or one similar to it: "Almighty, eternal God, give us an increase of Faith, Hope and Charity, and in order that we may deserve to obtain what Thou promisest, make us *love what Thou commandest.*"

VII.—Our Prayer must be Confident.

According to the Apostle St. James, one of the principal defects of prayer is a want of faith or a want of confidence in God that He will hear our prayer. "Let him who wavereth, that is he who has no confidence in the Lord, not think that when he prays he will receive anything of Him," says the Apostle. "A diffident prayer," says St. Bernard, "cannot enter into heaven, because immoderate fear restrains the soul so much, that when it prays it not only has no courage to raise itself to heaven, but it dares not even so much as stir. Now it hopes to be heard, then it doubts, saying to itself: "I shall obtain what I ask; no, I shall not. God will grant what I pray for; no, He will not do so, or He will do so when too late. He will give it sparingly. I deserve to be heard; no, I do not deserve it. I am worthy of it; no, I am unworthy of it. God is merciful and liberal, but He is a just God. His mercy is great, but my sins are too numerous and too great to be heard." Hence, it happens that in this fluctuation of thoughts and doubts, he at one time prays to God with patience, then complains of and murmurs against Him with impatience; again, he is resolved to wait until God is pleased to hear him; at another time he loses courage and feels angry, because he is not heard at once. Hence, he is, as St. James says, "like the waves of the sea, which are moved and carried about by the wind," giving himself up to these thoughts and doubts without making any serious effort to combat them; especially so when he meets with any trouble, adversity, cross or the like. Thus Moses began to doubt, on account of the unworthiness of the rebellious Jews, saying, "Hear ye rebellious and incredulous, can we bring you forth water out of this rock." (Numbers xx. 10.) In punishment for his want of confidence, he had to die in the desert. And the Lord said to Moses: "Because you have not believed Me, you shall not bring this people into the land which I will give them." St. Peter also, when walking upon the water at the command of Jesus, and perceiving the great wind, commenced to doubt and lose confidence in His word. Our Lord reproached him for it, saying: "O thou of little faith, why didst thou doubt?" (Matt. xiv. 31.) Hence, if we wish to be heard in prayer, we must, as the Apostle says, "pray with faith." But this faith to be good must have three qualities. First, it must be right faith in its true meaning,

18

free from hesitation or doubt, as otherwise it would be infidelity or heresy; secondly, it includes confidence, or certain, firm hope, free from diffidence or despair; and thirdly, it comprises a firm conviction of obtaining what we ask, excluding all wavering, or the fear and belief of not obtaining what we ask.

First. The Apostle St. James requires, for prayer, right faith in its true bearing, not only in general, that is to say, faith in God's omnipotence, providence, munificence, veracity, paternal care and love for us all; that as God, He is able, and as Father, inclined to do good to us, His children; but also in particular, that is, that He will give us what we ask, provided it be not detrimental to us. This is the very promise of Him Who is Truth itself, and can neither deceive nor be deceived: "And all things whatsoever you shall ask in prayer believing you shall receive." (Math. xxi. 22, Mark xi. 23, and elsewhere.) We believe with a divine faith that God is faithful to His promises, giving us what we ask of Him in prayer, and as it is impossible for God to deny Himself, so in like manner is it impossible for Him to break His promises. This faith our Lord often required of those who asked of Him their health or the like. To the blind, for instance, He said: "Do you believe that I can do this unto you?" And when they said: "Yea, Lord," He said to them: "According to your faith, be it done unto you: And their eyes were opened." (Math. xxviii. 29.)

Secondly. This faith produces hope and confidence, on which account St. Paul calls it "the substance of things to be hoped for," (Heb. xi. 1), because faith, in the omnipotence and veracity of God, is the strongest foundation and ground-pillar of hope, and of all things to be hoped for. For this reason, St. Augustine says: "If this faith is gone, prayer is gone with it." (Serm. 36, de verbo Dom.) It is for this very reason that the Apostle said, when exhorting to prayer: "Whosoever shall call upon the name of the Lord shall be saved" (Rom. x. 13), thus giving us to understand that prayer necessarily supposes, not only true faith, but also hope, by a natural consequence, because hope is the nurse of prayer. As a river will cease to flow if its source be dried up, so, in like manner there can be no longer any prayer, if its source, that is, hope and confidence have fled. This confidence was likewise demanded by Jesus Christ, when He said to the man sick of the palsy: "Be of good heart, son, thy sins are forgiven thee." (Math. ix. 2.) And again to the woman: "Be of good heart, daughter, thy faith hath made thee whole," (ver. xxii.), from which it is evident that Jesus Christ requires not only faith, but confidence, proceeding from faith. Hence, St. Thomas Aquinas says: "Prayer derives its efficacy of meriting from charity, but its efficacy of obtaining (impetrating) from faith and confidence," (2, 2, 9, 83, Art. 15 ad 3), as the Apostle St. James said.

Thirdly. As faith produces hope and confidence, so in like manner do these produce a certain persuasion in the mind, that God will grant what we ask of Him. Now, the greater the hope and the confidence of the heart, the stronger will be this persuasion in the understanding to obtain the grant of our prayer.

This three-fold faith makes prayer efficacious. It is, indeed, a great gift of the Lord to a soul, and almost a certain sign that He will hear its prayer, even though a miracle should be necessary to that effect. This is that wonder-working faith, that is, faith joined to a firm confidence in God's aid for the working of the miracle. This confidence is produced by an interior impulse of the grace of God, Who animates the Thaumaturgus (the performer of the miracle), promising him, as it were, His assistance for the miracle which he intends to work. Of this confidence Jesus Christ says : " Amen I say to you, if you shall have faith and stagger not, not only this of the fig-tree shall you do, but also if you shall say to this mountain, take up and cast thyself into the sea, it shall be done." " And all things whatsoever you shall shall ask in prayer, believing, you shall receive." (Math. xxi. 21-22.)

Now, in order to conceive great confidence, to increase it, and to become strengthened and confirmed in it, we must consider what God is in relation to us, and what we are in relation to Him.

First. What is God in relation to us? No one could tell this better than Jesus Christ, His well-beloved Son. "No one," said He, "knoweth who the Father is but the Son." (Luke x. 22.) Now, He has told us in distinct language, that "God is our Father." "Thus, therefore, shall you pray: 'Our Father Who art in heaven.'" (Matt. vi. 9.) "God is our Father," says Jesus Christ. But what kind of a Father is He? He is a Father Whose liberality surpasses all human understanding. What are we to consider in a father? It is the degree of fondness with which he communicates himself and all his goods, as far as possible, to his children. The greater this fondness is the greater will be his liberality. Now, God being our Father, there is in Him as such, unbounded fondness of communicating Himself. This infinite desire of communicating Himself is essential to God's nature, for God is infinite love; love, however, culminates in the reproduction of itself, that is, in generating its own image. Hence faith teaches us that God is Father, and as such, eternally generates another Himself (Self), Who is His Son, His most perfect Image; He, together with His Son, eternally generates a third Himself (Self), proceeding from both, Who is their reciprocal love—the Holy Ghost; so that the one and the same Divine Essence is quite the same in each of the three Divine Persons. But, as there can be no multiplication of the infinite simple Divine Essence, the infinite love which God has to Himself prompted Him to turn to what is not Himself, that is to say, to the creation of things, which are by Him, in Him, through Him, and yet are not Himself, that He might lavish upon them His perfections to a certain degree, but more especially so upon rational creatures, Angels and men, without ever diminishing Himself in the least, no matter how much He bestows upon them, and making them, at the same time, partake of His plenitude. As the sun, by sending forth its rays, exercises its influence over all nature, thus illuminating, warming and vivifying it, so God, in like manner, by sending forth the rays of His goodness upon all creatures, especially upon Angels and men, communicates Himself to them, illumining them by the light of His wisdom, that He may thereby inflame them with love of Himself, and vivify them by His grace and glory, and that they, too, in their turn, may impart it to others.

St. Dionysius says of Divine love : " That it is a power moving and drawing upwards to God, Who alone is good and perfect by Himself." We have evident proofs and effects of this love, beneficence and communion in the Incarnation of the Divine Word, for the purpose of teaching and saving mankind, in His Preaching, His Miracles, His Passion, His Death ; in the sending of the Holy Ghost ; in the Holy Sacraments, especially that of the Holy Eucharist, in which He may be said to have exhausted His Omnipotence, His Wisdom and His Love for man, as well as in His most wonderful care for His Church in general, and for each faithful soul in particular.

Again, in the justification and sanctification of every one, God not only communicates Himself to the soul by grace and charity, and other virtues, but also by Himself, giving, in reality, the Holy Ghost, and along with Him the other Divine Persons, according to St. Paul, writing to the Romans (v. 50): " The charity of God is poured forth in our hearts by the *Holy Ghost, Who is given to us ;*" and, " If any one love Me, he will keep My word, and My Father will love him, and We will come to him and will make Our abode with him." (John xiv. 23.) By thus communicating Himself, He raises the just man to Himself, transforming him into Himself, thus making him, as it were, divine, especially him who gives himself up to Him wholly and entirely, and without reserve. Divine love enraptures the loving soul, raising it above itself in order to transmute it into the beloved, and to unite it to Him most intimately ; to make it become *one* with Him, so that being, as it were, embodied in Him, it may live, feel and rejoice solely in Him alone. Thus the soul that truly loves God becomes entirely destitute of itself, passing over into God and dissolving, so to speak, into Him. It thinks, understands, feels only for God, desiring, seeking and rejoicing in His goods alone. He who thus adheres to God becomes but one spirit with Him, divesting himself entirely of self and putting on God, as if there were a transformation into the Divine Nature. Hence all his thoughts and affections are in God, he being of those for whom Christ asked when He prayed : "Holy Father, keep them in Thy name whom Thou hast given Me, that they may be one as We also are One" (John xvii. 11) ; and (vers. 21), "That they all may be one, as Thou, Father, in Me, and I in Thee, that they also may be one in Us." It must be observed that this communication and overflow of God's beneficence is prodigious and most wonderful, for five reasons :

First. On account of the greatness and majesty of the Lover and Giver ; for what can be greater or more sublime than God?

Secondly. On account of the condition of those to whom He communicates Himself with all His goods ; considered in their nature, they are men, the lowest of rational beings ; considered in the quality of their soul, they are proud, ungrateful, carnal sinners, incapable of doing any good, and prone to every evil ; considered in the quality of their body, they are but mortal, corrupt, vile and disgusting creatures, destined to be soon the food of worms. Thus did the Psalmist exclaim with truth :

"What is man that Thou art mindful of him, or the son of man, that Thou visitest him." (Ps. viii. 5.)

Thirdly. On account of the manifold and prodigious goods which He partly confers on them and partly offers them. These are a rational soul, created according to His own image and likeness, His grace, the promise of glory, the protection of His Angels, the whole visible world, and finally, His own well-beloved Son. "For God so loved the world as to give His only begotten Son; that whosoever believeth in Him may not perish, but may have life everlasting." (John iii. 16).

Fourthly. On account of the *end* for which He confers benefits; namely, for the happiness of man, not for His own happiness; for God does not expect to receive any gain or advantage from man.

Fifthly. On account of the manner in which He communicates and bestows Himself, which is also manifold.

First. Because it is peculiar to the divine benignity to lower itself to what is vile and despicable, to heal what is ailing, to seek what is rejected, to exalt what is humble, and to pour out His riches and His assistance where they are most needed.

Secondly. This feature of the divine benignity and care shines forth most strikingly and touchingly in the example of our first parents. When you hear them sharply reproved for having violated the command of God; when you hear their condemnation pronounced in this awful sentence: "Cursed is the earth in thy work: with labor and toil shalt thou eat thereof all the days of thy life: thorns and thistles shall it bring forth to thee; and thou shalt eat the herbs of the earth;" (Gen. iii. 17–18) when you see them driven out of Paradise; when you read that, to extinguish all hope of return, a fiery cherub was placed at the entrance, "brandishing a flaming sword, turning every way;" (Gen. iii. 23, 24), when you know that to avenge the injury done Him, God consigned to them every affliction of mind and body; when you see and know all this, would you not be led to pronounce that man irrevocably lost? That he was not only deprived of all assistance from God, but also abandoned to every species of misery? But although the storm of divine wrath burst over his guilty head, yet the love and benignity of God shot a gleam of consolation across the darkness which enveloped him. The sacred Scriptures inform us that "the Lord God made, for Adam and his wife, garments of skins and clothed them," (Gen. iii. 21), a most convincing proof that God, even when He seems to be angry, does not cease to pour out the inexhaustible treasures of His mercy.

Secondly. Because He often communicates Himself before He is asked, as He does in all the so-called preventing graces, by which He moves the soul to pray for subsequent ones ; for no one will pray to God in that manner in which he ought, says St. Augustine, unless he be incited to it by the grace of the Holy Ghost.

Thirdly. Even when the "Lord touches" (Job xix. 21), it is not with hostile purpose, but to heal by striking. If He chastises the sinner, it is to reclaim him by salutary severity, and rescue him from everlasting perdition by the infliction of present punishment. "He visits our iniquities with a rod, and our sins with stripes, but His mercy He taketh not away from us." (Ps. lxxxviii. 34.) "He woundeth and cureth: He striketh and His hand shall heal." (Job v. 18).

Fourthly. If asked, He gives more than is asked of Him. The good thief on the cross asked of Jesus Christ, no more than to be mindful of him in His kingdom, (Luke xxiii. 42,) but Jesus Christ gave him far more, saying to him : "Amen I say to thee, this day thou shalt be with Me in Paradise ;" "for grace," says St. Ambrose, "is always more abundant than prayer." King Ezechias prayed to God to restore his health, which the Lord was pleased to grant, and even much more, adding fifteen years to his life, and granting him a miraculous victory over the Assyrians. (Isai. xxxviii.) Solomon asks wisdom of the Lord, Who gave it him, besides immense wealth and riches. (III Kings iii.) Daniel prayed to God for the deliverance of the Jews from the Babylonian captivity, and the Lord revealed to him the time of the coming of the Messiah, Who was to deliver the whole world from the captivity of the devil. (Dan. ix. 24). David prayed for a son, and God promised him that the Messiah would descend from him. (II Kings vii. 12).

Fifthly. Because He often lavishes His gifts on those whom He foresees will be ungrateful; nay, even upon the impious, upon infidels, heretics, atheists, blasphemers and reprobates, according to what our Lord says in the Gospel: "Love your enemies; do good to them that hate you, etc., that you be the children of your Father, Who is in heaven, Who maketh the sun to rise upon the good and the bad, and raineth upon the just and the unjust." (Matt. v. 4, 5.) Who will dare deny, after these considerations, that God is, for us, the best, the kindest and most liberal of Fathers? Jesus Christ knew this but too well, and knowing, at the same time, that every one has most confidence in his own father, and that His heavenly Father wished us to have the greatest confidence in Him, especially when we pray, He wanted to call our attention to His relationship with us, to His infinite love, fondness and promptness of communicating Himself and all His gifts to us by saying: "Amen, amen, I say to you, if you ask the *Father* anything in My name, He will give it you." (John xvi. 23.) It is something quite remarkable, that our Lord Jesus Christ, when exhorting us to pray, would never use the expressions: "If you ask your Creator, your God, your Lord," and the like, but He always says: "If you ask the Father anything." God exhorts all men, by the wise man, "to be mindful of Him in the days of their youth." But in doing this, He does not use the expression "*Father*," but "Creator." "Remember thy Creator," He says, "in the days of thy youth." (Eccles. xii. 1.) If He reproaches His people with ingratitude, or reminds them of His benefits, He makes use of the title of "Redeemer" or "Saviour." "I am the Lord thy God, the Holy One of Israel, thy *Saviour*, I have given Egypt for thy atonement, Ethiopia and Saba for thee." (Isai. xliii. 3.) Whenever He gave commands to His people, He would say: "Thus saith the Lord," or, "the mouth of the Lord hath spoken it;" if threatening with punishments, He would say: "I will visit you, saith the Lord, with war, famine, pestilence, and then you shall know that I am your Lord and God." But whenever He speaks of prayer, and wants to be besought for His graces and gifts, He calls Himself (as I have just said), by the meekest, sweetest and most amiable name of "Father." Thus, therefore, shall you pray: "Our Father Who art in Heaven" (Matt. vi. 9); and again, "thou, when thou shalt enter into thy chamber, and having shut the door, pray to thy '*Father*' in secret, and thy '*Father*,' Who seeth in secret, will repay thee." (Matt. vi. 6.) At another time: " Amen, amen, I say to you, if you ask the *Father* anything in My name, He will give it you." (John xvi. 23; xv. 16; xiv. 13, 14.) And again: "If you, then, being evil, know how to give good gifts to your children, how much more will your *Father*, Who is in heaven, give good things to them that ask them." (Matt. vii. 11.) Behold, then, whenever our Lord Jesus Christ speaks of prayer, He intimates to us, on the part of His heavenly Father, that He wishes us to call Him, not by the title of " Almighty," or " Creator," or " Saviour," but by that of " Father." Why is this? First, because this name is, above all others, the most pleasing one we can give Him, and by calling Him " Father," we confer more honor upon Him than by any other appellation. According to St. Cyril, " it is something far greater in God to be *Father* than to be Lord, because, as Father, He generates His Son, Who is His consubstantial equal; but as Lord He made creatures, which are infinitely less than His Son." (Lib. I., Thesauri c. 6.) Secondly and principally, He wishes us to call Him by the name of Father, in order that we might have in Him, as our Father, the most perfect confidence in its widest acceptation. "Oh, the great dignity of a praying man, to have God for Father," exclaims St. Cajetan; " for you will not approach Him with your petition as a servant approaches his master, or a subject his prince, or a criminal his judge; no, you come to Him, like a child to his father, with love, and a firm confidence that nothing will be refused to you."

The Apostle, writing to the Romans, says: "You have not received the spirit of bondage again in fear, but you have received the spirit of adoption of sons, whereby we cry: Abba (Father)" (Rom. viii. 15), just like little children stretching forth their hands after their father, and crying: "Father"— an expression of the most tender love and affection, and of the most unbounded confidence. Certainly it would be the height of folly not to have confidence in one's own father. Were you to ask a favor of the President of the United States, and should he leave the grant of it to your father, would you hesitate for a moment to believe that your request would be complied with? Could the President give you a more favorable answer than by saying: "Go to your father, I will ratify *his* decision?" Oh, how kind is our Lord! As often as we pray for something, He points out to us His and our heavenly Father, Who is kindness, mercy, charity, liberality and love itself. It is to Him that we are to address our petition, saying: "Abba: Father." This word alone will touch His heart, in which love and mercy have taken up their abode. Absalom was a degenerated son, rebelling against David, his own father, and yet, how many and bitter were the tears which David shed when he heard of the death of his son. "The king, therefore, being much moved, went up to the high chamber over the gate, and wept; and as he went, he spoke in this manner: 'My son Absalom, Absalom; my son, who would grant me that I might die for thee. Absalom, my son; my son, Absalom.'" (II Kings xviii. 33.) But, holy king, over whom dost thou weep? Is it not over a rebellious son who intended to dethrone thee, to become king in thy stead? Now, has not his death been the means of thy deliverance? Shouldst thou not rather rejoice? St. Gregory, answering for him, says: "You cannot fathom the feelings of a father's heart. Absalom, it is true, was an impious son; but he was *my* son, whose death I deeply lament, and over which I am inconsolable."

The prodigal son also knew, but too well, how guilty he was in the sight of his father; yet, remembering the affectionate love of his father's heart, he felt quite consoled and full of confidence, and said to himself: "I will arise and will go to my father, and say to him: Father, I have sinned against heaven and before thee." (Luke xv. 18.) "How do you dare," asks St. Peter Chrysologus, "to go and see your father, against whom you have so much offended? What hope can you have to be received again?" And he answers: "He is my father. I have not behaved, it is true, like a good son, yet, for all that, my father's heart and love for me have not died away. His heart will speak for me far more powerfully than could my words. No sooner shall I have called him by the name of father than his heart will feel moved to the quick; I will go to him without fear." This being true, with how great a confidence ought we not, then, to pray to our heavenly Father, of Whom, Tertullian says, "that no one can ever equal Him in kindness, in amiability and liberality." He says of Himself, by the prophet Isaias: "Can a woman forget her infant so as not to have pity on the son of her womb? And if she should forget, yet will I not forget thee. Behold, I have graven thee in my hands." (Ch. xlix. 15, 16.) Jesus Christ assures us of the same, when He says: "And I say not to you, that I will ask the Father for you; for the Father Himself loveth you." (John xvi. 26, 27.) Now, let us suppose that we were all children of one father; that that father was in heaven, and that God would reveal to us that He would give him power to grant us anything we should ask— oh! with how great a confidence would we not pray to our father. Which of us, for a moment, would doubt that his prayers would be heard? No; every one would say: "My father loves me too much to refuse my prayer; I shall obtain whatever I ask of him." Yet, it will always be true that the love of our natural father, were it even to equal that of the Blessed Virgin Mary, would always be limited to a certain degree, because he is a creature. Now, if, nevertheless, our confidence would be exceedingly great in our natural father, how much greater ought it not to be in our heavenly Father, Whose power, goodness, liberality and love for us are infinite? Were you, then, not to pray with as much, nay, with far more confidence to your heavenly Father, you would certainly do Him a great injustice, believing Him, as it were, to be less powerful, less good, less liberal, and less affectionate towards you than your earthly father. Far be it from you ever to make yourself guilty of this great blasphemy.

If the relation which God bears to us must necessarily inspire us with the greatest possible confidence, the relation we bear to Him is not less calculated to do so, for, if He be our Father, then we are his children, and the laws of all nations, in accordance with those of nature, grant to children a holy right to, and claim upon, their father's goods, especially so if they were given to him to transmit them to his children. The following parable will illustrate this right of children: A poor man, by the name of Peter, came one day to his friend Paul, and exposed to him his great wants and troubles: "Dear friend," said he, "do you not know any one who could help me?" "Yes, I do," replied Paul.

QUALITIES OF PRAYER. 219

"Go to Mr. N .... he will help you." "I am afraid," said Peter, "to go to him on account of his elevated position." "You need not be afraid," said Paul, "because this gentleman is goodness, liberality and charity itself; he receives and listens to every one with the greatest affability. He even published a circular, some time ago, in which he styled himself 'the father of the poor,' inviting them all to come and make him acquainted with their wants; he never feels happier than when with the poor, to relieve them. He is exceedingly rich, so much so that I think he could provide for all the poor in the world. He had a most amiable and darling son, to whom he made over all his possessions; but his son died a short time ago. In his will, he instituted the poor, without any exception, as heirs to all his goods, leaving his father executor of his will. Hence it is that this gentleman, besides his natural affection for the poor, feels himself bound in conscience to give them whatsoever they need. There is no reason, then, why you should fear to go and call on him, for you will certainly receive what you want." Peter, hearing this, went quite confidently to this gentleman, and received whatever he needed. In this parable the poor man represents ourselves, and the rich lord thereof is God. He has published a circular recorded in Holy Scripture; it is as follows: "Every one that asketh, receiveth" (Luke xiii. 10); and, "all things whatsoever you shall ask in prayer, believing, you shall receive." (Matt. xxi. 22.) He also gave up everything to His Son Jesus: "All things are delivered up to Me by My Father." (Matt. xi. 27.) But His Son Jesus died, having made us heirs to all His merits and riches of divine grace and gifts, and His Father considers us as His dear children, who, in justice, claim the merits and graces of His Son. Our Lord Jesus Christ called our attention to this right of ours when He said: "If you ask the Father anything in My name He will give it to you." (John xvi. 23.) You must represent to your heavenly Father, He means to say, that He is your Father, and that you are His children, and have as such, according to all divine and human laws, an indisputable claim upon His goods. Your claim is also the greater as I, His Son, became man, suffered so much, and died so cruel and ignominious a death, for no other purpose than this: to merit for you all goods and all treasures of the Divine power, goodness and mercy. Not on account of your own merits and works are you to claim everything from Him, but for the sake of My merits, My virtues, My life, My sufferings, My death, My dignity, and the authority which I enjoy with Him, you must ask His graces. Represent this to Him and say: "Father, shouldst Thou not hear our prayers, certainly Thou wouldst give us reason to think that Thou dost not love Thy

Son, Who said : 'Whatsoever you shall ask the Father in My name, He will give it to you.' Shouldst Thou not do this, Thou wouldst give Him the lie, and make us believe, as it were, that His merits were not great enough to obtain everything for us; would this not be very injurious to His honor? Again, shouldst Thou not hear us, Thy justice will be accused for not giving us what Thy Son gained for us during thirty-three years of hard labor and sufferings. Alas, our Father, shall ever such accusations be brought against Thee? No; Thou wilt give a thousand times more to Thy children than they ask rather than give the least cause to think unbecomingly of Thy power, goodness, liberality and love for Thy well-beloved Son."

A Sister of Charity, in the time of the war, went to an officer of the United States army to obtain a pass to go South, saying : "Please give me a pass, for the love of God." "I have no love for God," replied the officer. "Give me one for the love of your wife," she asked again. "I have no love for my wife," answered the officer. "Give me one, then, for the love of your children," continued the good Sister. "I have no love for my children," was his reply. "Give me one for the love of your best friend." "I have no such friend," said the officer. "Well," said the Sister, "is there nothing in the world that is dear to you and which you love much? Please reflect a while." "O yes," said the officer, after a moment's reflection; "I have a dear little child that I love most tenderly." "Well, please then," said the Sister, "give me a pass for the love of this dear little child." At these words, the heart of the officer was touched, and he gave her a pass. Truly, should God have no more love for His beloved Son than this officer had for his little child, He would feel obliged to hear our prayer, addressed to Him in His Son's name, so as not to appear less good than man. Alas! my God and Father, for having compared Thy love for Thy Son to that of a father for his child—Thy love being infinite like Thyself—what favor and grace, then, couldst Thou refuse if asked in the name of Thy beloved Son? Thou didst hear the prayers of the Jews when they asked Thee anything in the name of Thy servants Abraham, Isaac and Jacob, and shall it be said that Thou wilt not hear a Christian if he asks anything of Thee in the name and for the sake of the merits of Thy beloved Son? True it is, and true it always will be, what St. John Chrysostom has said of the name of Thy Son: "So powerful, so efficacious, and of so great an authority is it with the Father, that, for the sake of His name alone, He grants the most wonderful things." Oh, great St. John Chrysostom! wonderful is your praise of the power of the name of Jesus. But were you to unite to all the Angels and Saints of heaven in describing its power, you could not say anything more wonderful in favor of it than what Jesus Christ has said of it in these few words : "Amen, amen, I say to you, *whatsoever* you ask the Father in *My name*, He will give it to you." My Father, He says, grants *everything, nothing excepted*, that is asked in My name, and in order that you may not hesitate in the least, and have no doubt whatever to believe My words, I swear to you that it is so: " Amen, amen, I say to you," " which words imply a solemn oath," as St. Augustine remarks. Who shall, then, after such a solemn promise of God, confirmed even by an oath on His part, continue to perform a diffident prayer, still wavering in the least hope of receiving what he asks of God, in the name of Jesus Christ? Who does not see, after all these considerations, that such a wavering, such a hesitation and doubt would imply a great injury to the omnipotence of God, as if not able to give ; to His goodness, as if not willing to give ; to His fidelity in promising, as if not caring about, or being bound to keep His promises? Most assuredly His Holiness and Goodness would forbid Him to make promises to us if He did not intend to fulfil them ; but, as they are made, our faith in His veracity must forbid us also to doubt them in the least, and we must, consequently, confide and hope firmly that He will hear our prayer, saying, with St. Alphonsus: " And for myself," says this Saint, "I speak the truth, I never feel greater consolation, nor a greater confidence of my salvation, than when I am praying to God and recommending myself to Him. And I think the same happens to all other believers; for the other signs of salvation are uncertain and unstable; but, that God hears the man who prays to Him with confidence, is an infallible truth, just as it is infallible that God cannot fail in His promises." (St. Alphonsus on Confidence in Prayer.) Nay, Jesus Christ, the Eternal Truth, has said, that he who has this faith and confidence in His name shall do even greater things than He Himself did: "Amen, amen, I say to you, he that believeth in Me, the works that I do, he also shall do, and *greater than these shall he do.*" (John xiv. 12.) By what means shall we do these greater things? By invoking His name and praying for them in this same name, in order that the Father may be glorified in the Son, as He Himself explains it in the same place when He says: "Whatsoever you shall ask the Father in My name, that will I do, that the Father may be glorified in the Son." I leave you, my dear Apostles, He means to say, and return to My Father; but, in place of my bodily presence, I leave and give to you the invocation of My name, in order that, by this invocation, you may ask and receive these greater things.

Do not say that it is presumption to believe that God should be bound to hear our prayers. It would, indeed, be presumption to believe that He is bound to hear us on account of our own merits; but considering the infinite fondness of God in communicating Himself with all His gifts to His rational creatures, and the most astonishing proofs of it, as described above; His relation to us as Father and ours to Him as children; the infinite merits of Jesus Christ; His solemn promise, confirmed by His own oath, to give us whatsoever we ask the Father in His name; considering all these reasons, we are, certainly, no more presumptuous in thus believing, than a poor man would be in believing and hoping that a rich and honest man would give him an old cast-off garment after promising to do so. A holy presumption it may be called indeed, which unhesitatingly and unshakably trusts in God's goodness; a presumption most pleasing to God, with which a servant of the Lord converses with His Divine Majesty.

St. Gregory Nazianzen relates of his sister Gorgonia, that her prayer was once quite presumptuous. Being one day attacked by a severe illness, she went to church and prayed there to God in a threatening manner, protesting that she would not leave His Altar before she should be restored to health.

Palladius relates of Paul the Hermit, that "one day he exorcised a young man who was possessed by an evil spirit. But, as the devil cursed all the time, saying: "You shall not make me leave this young man by whatever means you may adopt," the holy Hermit commenced to pray to God most earnestly : " Why, O Lord, dost Thou not command the devil to obey me ? For half a day already have I been praying and trying to cast him out, but all in vain ; but now, be assured, I am resolved neither to eat nor drink anything, but die of hunger, rather than to rise without seeing this young man delivered from the evil spirit." And behold, in the same moment, the devil left the young man, howling and crying, without ever returning.

Surius relates of St. Catherine of Sienna, that, after her mother had suddenly died, without receiving the last Sacraments, she commenced to pray with an unusual fervor and unlimited confidence in God, saying : "Is it thus, O Lord, that Thou keepest Thy promise, that none of our family should die an unhappy death ? How couldst Thou permit my mother to die without the last Sacraments? Hear, now, O Lord, I will not rise from this place before Thou hast restored my mother alive ;" and behold, her mother arose from the dead, and lived still for several years. If she prayed for anything else, for instance, for the conversion of a sinner, she would say : "My God, I will not let Thee alone until Thou hast granted my petition."

Most wonderful indeed is what St. Ananias obtained by his confident prayer. The king of Babylon had commanded the Christians to remove a mountain by means of their prayer, in proof of the truth of their faith, as otherwise he would put them to death, or force them to renounce their faith. It was useless to represent to him that it was to tempt God, to ask a miracle of Him without necessity, for the mere purpose of satisfying curiosity. The barbarous king could not be shaken in his resolve. St. Anauias, Bishop of Alexandria, hearing of the distress of the Christians, went to the king, and confiding in the promise of God to hear every prayer, said to him: "In order that you may know, O king, that the promises of the God Whom we worship are not false, behold, that big mountain which you wish should move from its place, shall not only move, but run even." Then raising his voice, he said: "In the name of that God Who has promised us the obedience of the mountains, I command thee to rise and move towards the city, and do so all at once." No sooner had he spoken these words than he mountain rose, in the presence of the king and people, and moved towards the city as fast as a vessel, with a fair wind, on the ocean." (Petr. de nat. in Cat. Sanct. I. 9. c. 19.) It knocked down the trees and the houses, and the king, commencing to fear it might come upon the city, and destroy it altogether, requested the holy Bishop to stop the mountain in its course. The Saint did so, and the mountain again obeyed his voice, staying there up to this day.

With similar confidence in God, St. John the Almoner used to say: "Should all men of the whole world come to Alexandria to beg alms, I would give every one, for the whole world is not able to diminish or exhaust the treasures of God." Hence God would change brass into silver for him, and give him the hundredfold even in this life, so much so that the more he would spend the more he would receive." (His life by Leontius.)

Let us learn from this that God cannot refuse a confident prayer. Our hope and confidence are, as it were, the money with which we purchase all His graces, for we have nothing else to offer Him. He Himself values this confidence exceedingly, because He feels Himself extremely honored by it. By it we show that we distrust ourselves; that we stand in need of Him; that He is almighty, most merciful and most liberal; nay, even that He is God, Father, Ruler and Provider of ourselves, as well as of all His creatures. Hence His gifts stand in an exact proportion to our hope and confidence in Him. We shall most assuredly receive what we most confidently pray for. Hope and pray for great things, and great things shall be given you. The more room you make for confidence in your soul, the more you enlarge and prepare it for the reception of the gifts of God, according to what holy David says: "Open thy mouth wide and I will fill it." (Ps. lxxx. 11.) Whenever you go to prayer, reanimate your confidence in the Lord by calling to mind His infinite desire of communicating Himself and all His gifts to every one. Remember the stupendous effects of this desire in all that God has done through His Son ; do not forget His relation, as Father to you, and yours as a child to Him ; bear in mind His infallible promise to give whatsoever is asked in the name of Jesus Christ; do not lose sight of the confidence with which the Saints would pray to Him, and obtain most wondrous things. Imagine you hear, as it were, the voice of Jesus Christ whispering into your ear : " Whatsoever you ask, believing, you shall receive ;" or saying, as it did one day to the mother of St. Gregory of Tours, who was weeping bitterly, believing, as she did, that every member of the family would die of the epidemic which had widely spread in the city of Arveon : " Pray," said the voice, "and you shall be delivered." (St. Greg. Touron. apud Luc. in vit. St. Benigni.) She went to the grave of St. Benignus, and obtained there, by her fervent and confident prayer, the grace that none of her family should be attacked by the epidemic. Yes, pray ; but pray with confidence and you shall be delivered from all the miseries of your soul ; from darkness and blindness of the understanding ; from weakness and lethargy of the will ; from lukewarmness of the heart ; from coldness towards Jesus Christ. You will be delivered from

20*

your feebleness of faith in the sacred mysteries of our holy religion ; from tepidity and indevotion in your prayers and other spiritual exercises ; from attachment to sensual pleasures ; from sins and punishments due to them. Pray with confidence, and confident prayer will deliver you from all these and many other evils of the soul ; nay, it will do more, it will introduce into your soul all graces, gifts and virtues in an eminent degree ; for " Behold, the hand of the Lord is not shortened that it cannot save, neither is His ear heavy that it cannot hear" (Isai. lix. 1) ; or, as Jesus Christ says : " I tell you, God is able of these stones to raise up children to Abraham." (Matt. iii. 9.) Can you doubt this truth without being guilty of blasphemy ? Was He not able, and did He not change the heart of Saul, who was such a bitter enemy of the Catholic Church, into the heart of Paul, the most zealous defender and propagator of the holy faith ? Could He not, and did He not change the sinful heart of the good thief; of St. Augustine ; of St. Mary of Egypt ; St. Margaret of Cortona, and thousands of infidels, Jews, heretics and sinners, into most just and holy hearts, replenishing them with all His gifts and the treasures of His grace ? Will He not, and must He not, do the same for you, especially so, as He made an express promise to give this very grace, when He said : " If you, then, being evil, know how to give good gifts to your children, how much more will your Father from heaven *give the good Spirit to them that ask Him?*" (Luke xi. 13.) "Hitherto you have not asked anything, especially this good Spirit, in My name. Ask and you shall receive, that your joy may be full." (John xvi. 24.)

VIII.—Our Prayer must be Persevering.

When Holofernes was besieging the city of Bethulia, so that none could escape, all, men, women and children, young and old, commenced to pray and to fast, crying to the Lord, with tears in their eyes: "Have Thou mercy on us, because Thou art good." (Judith vii. 20.) But the Lord deferring to come to their aid, they began to yield to despair. Ozias, their leader, rising up all in tears, said: "Be of good courage, my brethren, and let us wait for these five days for mercy from the Lord ; but if, after five days be past, there comes no aid, we will do the things which you have spoken," that is, deliver up the city into the hands of the enemy, if, after having prayed for five days more, we have not yet received any aid from the Lord. Now, it came to pass that, when Judith heard of this, she came out and said to them : "What is this word by which Ozias hath consented to give up the city to the Assyrians, if, within five days, there come no aid to us?

And who are you that tempt the Lord, and you have appointed Him a day, according to your pleasure?" (Judith viii. 10, 11, 13.) Thus Judith reproaches the Jews and their leader for their rashness of having fixed upon the time within which God was to come to their aid. This is not the way to obtain mercy from God, but rather to excite His indignation; "this is not a word that may draw down mercy, but rather that may stir up wrath and enkindle indignation." (Judith viii. 12.)

Jesus Christ has, it is true, promised to give us everything we ask of Him, but He has not promised to hear our prayers immediately. The holy Fathers assign many reasons for which He often defers the grant of our petitions:

First. That He may the better try our confidence in Him.

Secondly. That we may long more ardently for His gifts and hold them in higher esteem. " He defers the grant of them," says St. Augustine, "in order to increase our desire and appreciation of them."

Thirdly. "That He may keep us near Him," as St. Francis de Sales says, " and give us occasion to pray with greater fervor and vehemence. He acted thus towards His two disciples at Emmaus, with whom He did not seem willing to stay, before they forced Him, as it were, to do so."

Fourthly. He delays, because by this contrivance, He wishes to unite Himself more closely to us. "This continual recourse to God in prayer," says St. Alphonsus, "and this confident expectation of the graces which we wish to obtain from God, oh! what a great spur and chain of love are they not to inflame us and to bind us more closely to God!" We must not, therefore, imitate the Jews by appointing the time within which God is to hear our prayer, as otherwise we would deserve the above reproach of Judith, but let us humble ourselves before the Lord, and pray to Him with tears that *according to His will,* so He would show His mercy to us." (Judith viii. 16, 17.) If we are patient, resigned and determined to persevere in prayer until He is pleased to hear us, we shall not be disappointed in our hope and expectation to receive what we ask of Him. Our Lord Jesus Christ taught us this when He said : " Ask and you shall receive ; seek and you shall find ; knock and it shall be opened to you." (Luke xi. 9.) It might seem that He would have said enough, by simply saying "*Ask*," and that the words "seek" and "knock" would be superfluous. "But no," says St. Alphonsus, "by them our Saviour gave us to understand, that we must imitate the poor when they ask alms. If they do not receive the alms they ask they do not, on that account, cease asking ; they return to ask again ; and if the master of the house does not show himself, they commence to *knock* at the door, until they become so troublesome and importunate that he prefers to give them an alms, rather than to suffer their importunity any longer." If we pray, again and again in like manner, and do not give up, God will, at last, open His hands and give us abundantly. "When Thou openest Thy hand they shall all be filled with good." (Ps. ciii. 28).

If men sometimes give alms to poor beggars, merely for the sake of ridding themselves of their importunity and annoyances, "how much more," says St. Augustine, "will the good God give, Who both commands us, and is angry if we do not ask." Hence St. Jerome, commenting on the parable of the man who would not give his loaves to his friend in the middle of the night, until he became importunate and annoying in his demands, says: "Not only once, but twice, yea, three times must we knock, and we must continue to do so, until the door of God's mercy be opened." Perseverance is a great thing; if it becomes importunate it will prove a better friend to us than the one mentioned in the parable.

"Let us humbly wait for the consolations of the Lord our God," (Judith viii. 20), and imitate the perseverance of the servants of God in prayer. Moses was a very great servant of the Lord, Who would not have granted him a complete victory over the Amalekites, had it not been for his perseverance in prayer. "By perseverance in prayer," says St. John Chrysostom (in his sermon on Moses), "he rendered the victory complete." Isaac was very dear to the Lord, and yet, in order to obtain an offspring, he had to pray for twenty years. "Isaac persevered in praying and sighing to the Lord for twenty years," says the same Saint, "and finally he obtained what he asked." (Hom. 94 in Gen.) And how did the Lord treat the woman of Canaan? "And behold a woman of Canaan, who came out of those coasts, crying out and said to Him: " Have mercy on me, O Lord, Thou Son of David; my daughter is grievously troubled by a devil." (Matt. xv. 22.) And what does our Lord reply? He does not even as much as look at her, nor does He give her any answer, "Who answered her not a word." Still she continues to pray with great humility: "Lord, help me." But our Lord seems not to hear her, so much so, that even His disciples, being wearied and annoyed with her supplication, "came and besought Him saying: Send her away for she crieth after us." Instead of hearing her, He rejects her like a dog, saying: "It is not good to take the bread of the children, and to cast it to the dogs." Who can discover in this conduct of our Lord, anything of His usual kindness and condescension, which He would deign to show even to the greatest sinners? Will He not, by His manner of acting, intimidate or discourage this woman, so as to make her give up all hopes of being heard? But no, Jesus Christ had His own wise designs in thus treating her. He knew her and was much pleased with her faith and confidence, which He wanted to make shine forth more brilliantly. "But she said : Yea, Lord, for the whelps also eat of the crumbs that fall from the table of their masters." True, indeed, she wished to say, I am but a poor dog, but, as such, I beg to help me, O Lord. And the liberal hand of Jesus opens and gives her what she wants. "Then Jesus answering, said to her: O woman, great is thy faith : be it done to thee as thou wilt ; and her daughter was cured from that hour." Had this woman been satisfied with the first answer of our Lord, her daughter would never have been cured. St. Monica (mother of St. Augustine) was treated in like manner; she had to pray to God for seventeen years before she could obtain of Him the grace of conversion for her son Augustine. Had she become tired with pouring out prayers and shedding tears before the face of the Lord, in all probability the name of Augustine would not now be shining with such great lustre in the calendar of the Saints. For twenty years did St. Philip Neri pray for a high degree of the love of God. After that time this gift was granted him in such a measure as to dislocate his ribs.

Not only the servants of God, but even Jesus Christ Himself was thus treated by His heavenly Father. Prostrate on His face, He prays to Him, but receives neither relief nor comfort. He prays a second time in a most lamentable voice: "Father, if it be possible, let this chalice pass away from Me"—neither is He heard this time. He prays a third time with greater intensity, and not till then did the Angel come to comfort and strengthen Him.

Poor miserable creatures, wretched sinners as we are! What an exalted opinion have we not of ourselves! The heavenly Father lets His only begotten, well-beloved, most innocent and afflicted Son, like a poor beggar, knock three times at His door, before He opens—and we think we have done enough when we have petitioned a few times at the gate of heaven! We so readily complain of being unmercifully treated by God if He does not come at once to our aid, and despairing, as it were, of being heard, we give up praying altogether. "Truly, this is not the right way to pray," says St. John Chrysostom; "let us bewail our indolence in praying; for thirty-eight years had the sick man, spoken of in the Gospel, (John chap. iv.), waited to be cured, and yet his desire had not been accomplished. Nor had it happened thus through his negligence; yet, for all that, he did not despair; but if we pray for ten days perhaps, and are not heard, we think it is of no use to pray any longer." (Homil. 35, in Joan.)

We must then follow the advice of St. Gregory, when he comments on, (Ps. cxxix.), "Let us be assiduous in prayer, and importunate in asking ; let us beware of growing remiss in it, when it appears the Lord will not hear us; let us be robbers, as it were, doing violence to heaven. What robbery can be more meritorious, what violence more glorious? Happy violence by which God is not offended, but appeased, by which sin is not multiplied, but diminished." If we wish, then, to pray aright, we must not only commence to pray but must also continue our prayer, especially if we ask something conducive to our own spiritual welfare, or to that of our neighbor. Most of men fail in this point, and this is the reason why their prayer is of such little efficacy. Never allow yourself to become guilty of voluntary despondency. " Keep firm to the promise of Jesus Christ," says St. John Chrysostom ; "never cease praying until you have received. If you present yourself before the Lord with this firm determination, saying : "I will not leave Thee till Thou hast granted my prayer, you will receive most assuredly." (Hom. 24, in Mass, c. vii.) Let us say with the Apostle: " Why should I not be able to do what others have done?" What so many could obtain by their perseverance in prayer, why should we not be able, by our perseverance, to obtain whatsoever we ask ? What a shame will it not be for us to see, on the judgment-day, how the Saints of heaven, by their perseverance in prayer, have become what they are, whilst we, for our want of

QUALITIES OF PRAYER. 239

perseverance in prayer, shall appear so very unlike unto them! Most assuredly, Almighty God will manifest His power, goodness and mercy in us, as much as He has done in all the Saints, provided we pray for it with the perseverance of the Saints.

CHAPTER

HOW TO ACQUIRE THE SPIRIT OF PRAYER.

"I will pour out upon the house of David, and upon the inhabitants of Jerusalem, the spirit of grace and of prayers."
[ZACHARIAS xii. 10.

AFTER having heard so much of the efficacy and advantages of prayer, you must doubtless be anxious to know how you can acquire that spirit of prayer which the Saints possessed, and which the Lord promised to pour out upon the inhabitants of Jerusalem. I answer, as St. Francis de Sales did when asked what one should do to obtain the love of God: "We must love Him," said he; so in the same way, I say, we must pray in order to learn how to pray. No art, no language, no trade can be learned without the practice of it; so prayer, too, must be learned by the frequent exercise thereof. It was in this way the Saints obtained the spirit of prayer. St. Teresa was accustomed to offer herself to God fifty times in the day. St. Martha used to pray, kneeling one hundred times in the day and one hundred times in the night. St. Francis Borgias also was accustomed to pray, kneeling one hundred times in the day. St. Philip Neri made a kind of rosary of the words which the Church uses in reciting the Divine Office: "O God, come to my aid; O Lord, make haste to help me." He recited this rosary sixty-three times in the day, and enjoined his penitents to do the same. St. Gertrude repeated the third petition of the "Our Father": "Thy will be done on earth as it is in heaven," three hundred and sixty-five times a day. Blessed Leonard of Port Maurice, recommended himself to the Blessed Virgin Mary two hundred times in the day. We read of St. Francis de Sales, that by means of very frequent ejaculatory prayers, he always kept himself in the presence of God, even amidst his many pressing occupations. Blessed Brother Gerard was often beaten by his foreman who could not endure to see him praying even whilst at work. It is related of St. Elizabeth of Hungary, that when she played as a young girl, with other children of her age, and her turn came to sit down and rest, she would profit by these leisure moments to say a "Hail Mary." Of another Saint, it is related, that for thirty years he said no other prayer than "Lord, have mercy on me!" and at the end of this time the Lord poured out His mercy upon him most abundantly, bestowing on him a high degree of contemplation, and raising him to a state of eminent sanctity. Blessed Leonard of Port Maurice used to say, we should not allow a moment to pass without repeating the words: "Have mercy on me! oh Jesus, have mercy on me!" He relates that he knew a man who repeated this prayer: "Jesus, have mercy on me!" three hundred times in a quarter of an hour. We read of the Apostle St. Bartholomew that he used to offer to God two hundred adorations daily. In the Roman Breviary we read of St. Patrick, that when guarding the cattle, he prayed to God a hundred times in the day and a hundred times in the night, and when a Bishop, he daily said the psalter, containing one hundred and fifty psalms, and many canticles and hymns, besides two hundred other different prayers; he also made three hundred genuflections every day, in adoration of the Blessed Trinity, and the sign of the cross one hundred times at each canonical hour. Before St. Margaret of Cortona had attained to contemplation, her devout exercises consisted simply of Pater Nosters; but so many were they in number, that they daily exceeded a thousand. She said three hundred in honor of the Blessed Trinity; one hundred in honor of the great Mother of God; one hundred for each of her kindred most beloved by her; one hundred for her sins; one hundred for the Franciscan Order; one hundred for the people of Cortona; one hundred for those who injured her, and many hundred more for the Sovereign Pontiff, for all ecclesiastical orders, for sinners, heretics, schismatics, Turks, Jews, etc. St. Alphonsus, before going to sleep, would make the following good acts: Ten acts of love; ten acts of confidence; ten acts of sorrow; ten acts of conformity to the will of God; ten acts of love to Jesus Christ; ten acts of love to the Blessed Virgin; ten acts of love to Jesus in the Blessed Sacrament; ten acts of confidence in Jesus Christ; ten acts of confidence in the Blessed Virgin; ten acts of resignation to suffering; ten acts of abandonment to God; ten acts of abandonment to Jesus Christ; ten acts of abandonment to Mary, and ten prayers to know and do the will of God. If this Saint made so many good acts previous to going to bed, how many must he not have made in the course of the entire day? But how is it possible, you will say, for one to pray so much in the course of the day? St. Alphonsus answers: "Give me a soul that truly loves God, and it will tell you." It is easy for love to think of the Beloved and to converse frequently and familiarly with Him. But I cannot pray, you will say, as much as the Saints did; it would be necessary for me to be a Saint myself; if I cannot acquire the spirit of prayer unless I do as much as they did, I give up all hope of ever obtaining it. Do not be alarmed, but remember that neither did the Saints know all at once how to pray so well and so much; most of them learned it by slow degrees. The practice of prayer was not familiar to them in the beginning; but, perseveringly increasing it, they gradually acquired that great facility which raised them to contemplation. As the speaking of a language, the exercise of a trade, or an art, become more easy in proportion to the practice of them, so does the practice and exercise of prayer, The following example is a striking illustration of this: Father Pergmayr, S. J., relates in his writings, vol. 3, of Father Didaues Martinez, S. J., famous for his sanctity, many miracles and thousands of conversions wrought among the heathens in Peru, that this holy man was so constantly united with God that he would spend whole nights in prayer, in the open air, in which God communicated Himself so much to him that this Apostle of the Lord would often be seen raised in the air above the highest trees, surrounded by a heavenly splendor, between two columns of fire. But he was not satisfied with this prayer of the night, and being overburdened with labor during the day, he satisfied his great ardor for prayer by constant ejaculations, which became so frequent that they exceeded four thousand, sometimes even five thousand a day. He attained to this great union with God by a small beginning. On entering the novitiate, he resolved to raise his heart to God seven times in the day. After awhile he increased this number of ejaculations to one hundred, and before the end of his novitiate, to five hundred every day. At last this manner of praying became so familiar to him that his ejaculations were from four to five thousand every day.

Rest assured that most of the Saints made use of frequent ejaculations of the heart as one of the most efficacious means to acquire the spirit of prayer, though there is no mention made of it in their lives; and you, too, will be greatly advanced in the spirit of prayer by this means, provided you use it as the Saints did, with increasing fervor and perseverance. But how can I, you will say, count my ejaculations and aspirations of the heart? It is too troublesome! I answer, if you truly love your soul, you will soon find out a way to count them, just as well as a merchant knows how to count every cent he spends or receives. For this purpose you can make use of beads like those of St. Philip Neri, or you can count your ejaculations by the hours of the day, making a stated number of them during each hour; for until you have acquired the salutary and holy habit of praying everywhere and always, it will be advisable for you to count your ejaculations, in order to be confident whether you advance or retrograde in prayer. Should you have resolved to say seven times in the day, the "Our Father;" or, "Lord, come to my aid;" or, "Jesus, have mercy on me;" or, "Lord, Thy holy will be done;" or, "*Lord, do as Thou pleasest with me;*" or, "Jesus, make me love Thee more and more;" or, "Jesus, pour out upon me the spirit of prayer," or some other aspiration with which you may be inspired, you should be careful to make the number of ejaculations you have enjoined on yourself, and when you have acquired a facility in making the proposed number in an hour, increase this number by five, and after having succeeded in regularly making twelve an hour, increase again this number, and so go on until this manner of prayer has become a second nature to you, as it were, and an indispensable want of your soul. Should you, in the beginning, be unable to make these ejaculatory prayers with the heart only, be careful to make them with the fervor of the will, and by degrees you will, like the Saints, pass from vocal prayer to a better and easier kind of prayer, viz: that of the heart. And in order the sooner to accomplish this, you must imitate a person who wishes to learn a language or music in a short time. Now what does this person do to succeed in his design? He refrains from everything that does not positively concern him, caring only for what he so much desires soon to learn and understand; to this all his thoughts are directed day and night. Now, if you wish to learn in a short time how to pray well, you, too, must let everything alone that is not your business, caring and striving only to learn the science of the Saints. It is certainly not your business to gratify your natural inclinations, desires and passions; therefore let them alone. To attach your heart to the enjoyments, comforts and pleasures of this world is surely not your business; therefore, refrain from them. To wish to be praised, honored and to do your own will in everything, is not your business; therefore mortify this desire; otherwise your case will be the same as that of a man who undertakes all sorts of business, and succeeds in none of them perfectly, because the one is an obstacle to the good success of the other. To wish to hear, to see and to enjoy everything in this world—to love and esteem all that it loves and esteems, is to put great obstacles in the way of your sanctification and of acquiring that spirit of prayer which the Saints possessed; you will always have to complain of having but little desire to pray, and of feeling a great reluctance to prayer, of performing it with much lukewarmness, with many distractions, of almost despairing of any success or progress in it, but no one will be able to afford you any consolation as long as you do not make serious endeavors to detach your heart from everything in this world. Can you press sweet cider from sour apples, gather grapes from thorns, or figs from thistles? Such as is the corn put into the mill, such, also, will be the flour. In vain do we expect our heart to conceive many holy desires and produce fervent aspirations and ejaculatory prayers, if it is continually occupied with vain and frivolous objects, wholly unworthy of the heart and soul of a Christian. As a farmer will reap what he has sowed, so will your heart and mind be occupied in the time of prayer with those worldly objects for which you cherish any disorderly affection. Your heart will be where your treasure is, says our Lord in the Gospel. The devil, well aware of this truth, in order to prevent you from praying, or from making any essential progress in this most sublime occupation of man, does all in his power to present your "Benjamin" your most beloved object to your mind at the time of prayer. A superintendent of a very important work will always endeavor to prevent, as much as possible, all his workmen from talking to others, or from doing anything but what he tells them to do. You, too, must forbid your heart and mind to be occupied with what does not concern you, and to apply only to the acquisition of the spirit of prayer. Forbid all your Benjamins to speak to you in this holy exercise. Be determined and inexorable not to permit it, imitating Count

Rougemont, of whom St. Vincent de Paul relates the following: "I knew," he says, "in the Province of Bresse the Chevalier Rougemont, who was once so famous for his duels, in which he had wounded and killed an almost incredible number. After his conversion to a very edifying life, I had the pleasure of visiting him at his own residence, where he commenced to speak to me about his devout exercises and practices of virtue, and among others, of his complete independence of and detachment from creatures. "I feel assured," said he to me, "that if I am perfectly detached from creatures, I will be most perfectly united to my Lord and God; for this reason I often examine my conscience, asking myself if there is anything to which I feel any attachment, whether to myself, to my relatives, friends or neighbors; to the riches and comforts of life; to any passion or disorderly desire whatsoever that might prevent me from being perfectly united to and resting entirely in God alone. I commence to pray to God to enable me to cut down and root out at once whatever I notice to be an obstacle to my perfect union with Him." "I remember," continues the Saint, "a remarkable act of his, which he himself related to me, which shows how earnestly he went to work to gain a complete detachment from everything, and which I can never think of without admiration. As he was riding along on horseback one day, he stopped to reflect and find out whether, after he had made an oblation of himself to God, there was still something to which he might have at least some trivial attachment. After having most carefully examined all his occupations, recreations, honors and even the least affections and inclinations of his heart, he noticed his sword, for which he still entertained some affection. Why do you wear this sword? he said to himself. But what evil has it done you? Leave it where it is! It has rendered you many great services, and enabled you to save yourself in thousands of dangers. Should you again be attacked, without it, surely, you will be lost. But should you again have the occasion of a quarrel, would you have the self-command to keep it where it is, and not offend God again by the abuse of this sword? My God! what must I do? Shall I still love the instrument of my confusion and of so many sins? Alas! I see, my heart is yet attached to this sword! So mean I will not be, as to allow myself to be overcome by this miserable instrument! This said, he alighted from his horse, took a stone and broke his sword into pieces. He acknowledged to me that by this heroic victory over himself he felt his heart completely detached from everything, caring no more for anything in this world and feeling most powerfully drawn to love God alone above all things. Behold, gentlemen, said St. Vincent in conclusion, how happy we should be, and what progress we should make in virtue if, like this nobleman, we would purify our hearts from all earthly affections. If our hearts were completely detached from all creatures, how soon would our souls be united to God." Your facility in prayer and your attraction for it will increase in proportion to the efforts you make to detach yourself from all earthly things, especially from yourself. All the Saints have experienced and acknowledged this truth. Christoph Gonzalve, S. J., a disciple of blessed Balthazar Alvarez, was asked one day by a companion by what means he had obtained the extraordinary gift of prayer; he answered : " This did not cost me very much, I had only to follow the inspirations of God, to mortify and renounce entirely my desire of vain glory in scientific matters." He commenced his philosophical studies with an unusual facility, by which means he gained a great preeminence over all his companions. This superiority was a strong lever to ambition and a source of constant temptation to him, and in order to escape these dangerous snares securely, he adopted the following means without, however, neglecting his studies: to cause his companions to lose the high opinion they had of his superior talents, he would often ask them an explanation of certain points which he really understood better than they did. In controversies, he would give his opinion, but appeared to be at a loss how to corroborate it; when objections were made he would answer the first, but for the second he would pretend to have no answer; the consequence was that his professors would give the most difficult and most honorable thesis to others, and to him what was very easy and not procuring any honor; this was what he desired and aimed at. By this artifice of humility, of which his professors as well as his companions were ignorant, he lost with them all his renown for superiority of talents, and he gained a complete victory over self-love and ambition, in recompense for which God bestowed upon him the inestimable gift of sublime contemplation and great familiarity with Him in prayer. Thus it is true what the Lord said by the Prophet Isaias: "If thou turn away thy foot from doing thy own will, . . . thou shalt be delighted in the Lord, and I will lift thee up above the high places of the earth and will feed thee with the inheritance of Jacob thy Father. For the mouth of the Lord hath spoken it. (Isaias lviii. 13, 14.) Now, this promise of the Lord will come true in your regard also, provided you comply with the conditions, viz: to purify your heart from all attachment to earthly enjoyments, ambitions, and desires, but especially from all attachment to your own will and judgment. "Yes," says St. Francis de Sales, "God is ready to grant you the gift of prayer as soon as He sees you empty of your own self-will. If you are very humble, He will not fail to pour it out upon your soul. God will fill your vessel with His ointments as soon as it is empty of the ointments of this world, that is as soon as every desire of yours for earthly objects has made room for that of serving and loving Him alone."

The use of frequent and fervent ejaculatory prayers, and the complete detachment of your heart from all creatures are, it is true, most powerful means to acquire the spirit of prayer, but in order more quickly to obtain this inexpressible gift, we must frequently beg it of God; for this grace of prayer is, according to St. Francis de Sales, no water of this earth, but of heaven, therefore we cannot obtain it by any effort of our own; although it is true we should dispose ourselves for the reception of it with the greatest care. This care should, indeed, be great, but humble and calm. We must keep our heart open, waiting for the fall of this heavenly dew, and it will fall so much the sooner the more earnestly and perseveringly we pray and sigh for it every day, especially while assisting at the divine sacrifice of Mass, receiving holy Communion and visiting our most loving Lord in the adorable sacrament of the Altar, saying to Him: " Lord, teach me how to pray; grant me the spirit of prayer, and a great love for this holy exercise; make me often think of Thee, and find my greatest pleasure and happiness in conversing with Thee; let everything of this world become disgustful to me." The more frequently and earnestly you make these, or similar petitions to obtain the spirit of prayer, the more you will receive of this inestimable gift of the Lord, according to the infallible promise of Jesus Christ,—"All things whatsoever you ask in prayer, believing, you shall receive." (Matt. xxi. 22.) Continue thus asking until the Lord accomplishes in you what He has promised by the Prophet Zacharias: "I will pour out upon the house of David and upon the inhabitants of Jerusalem the spirit of grace and of prayers." (Chap. xii. 10). You clearly perceive from these words of the Prophet, that this gift of prayer is the spirit and gift of the Lord; you must, then, endeavor to obtain it, more by asking it of the Lord with great humility, fervor, confidence and perseverance, than by imprudent efforts of the brain and mind. Wait patiently for the hour, but do not neglect to do at the same time, what has been said in this chapter, and then rest assured that the moment will come in which the conversation with God will be easier, and more familiar to you than the conversation with your most intimate friend, and you will exclaim, with St. Augustine: "What is more excellent, more profitable, more sublime and sweeter for the soul, than prayer." You will, with Fathers Sanchez and Suarez, of the Society of Jesus, prefer the loss of all temporal goods to that of one hour of prayer, for then will be realized in you, what St. Paul says in his epistle to the Romans: "The Spirit also helpeth our infirmity; for we know not what we should pray for as we ought, but the Spirit Himself asketh for us with unspeakable groanings." (Chap. viii. 26.) Then the Holy Ghost Himself will pray in you and with you, inspiring such petitions and sighs as are pleasing to and heard by Him. And when the Lord, in His great mercy, has granted you this admirable gift, daily return Him thanks for it, and profit by it, both for your own temporal and spiritual welfare, and that of others, because this is God's will. Say often with the psalmist: " Take not Thy holy Spirit from me." (Ps. 1. 13.) Lord, never withdraw from me this spirit of grace and prayer, send me any other punishment for my sins rather than this. I repeat again, never forget to be thankful for this gift, always remembering that you can never fully understand or sufficiently appreciate it until after death ; for in it are included all the gifts and graces of the Lord. For this reason you must be very desirous to obtain it, and take every possible means to acquire it; and should you not have this ardent desire for it, you must beg it of God with great fervor and perseverance ; you should not take less pains, care and trouble, or make less efforts to obtain this great gift from God, than a good student does to learn a language, an architect to erect a costly and splendid edifice, or a general to gain the victory in an important battle. Would to God you understood this great and inestimable grace as perfectly and clearly as the devil does, I think you would take as much trouble to acquire it, and to preserve it when acquired, as he does to prevent you from receiving it, and make you lose it when in possession of it.

This sworn arch-enemy of our eternal happiness will suffer you to perform any kind of good works, such as fasting, scourging yourself, wearing haircloths, etc., rather than see you striving to advance in the way of prayer; the least time you spend in it is for him an insupportable torment. Although he leaves you quiet at all other times, rest assured that in the time of prayer he will use all his power to distract and disturb you in some way or other. In order to prevent you from praying well, he will fill your mind with thoughts and imaginations of the strangest and most curious kind, so much so, that what you would never think of at any other time will come to your mind at the time of prayer, in such a manner even that it would seem you came to prayer for no other purpose than to be distracted and assaulted by a whole army of the most frightful temptations, or he will make you feel peevish, and try to persuade you that prayer is the business of old women who have nothing else to do, but as for you that it is only a loss of time, which could be spent much more profitably in some other way. If you are a priest, a religious, or a student of theology, he will artfully represent to you how necessary and profitable it is to possess great learning, for the salvation of souls and the greater honor and glory of God, in order that the application to study may become your principal occupation, and that you may consider prayer as something merely accessory. If a Superior in a conference, a Confessor in the confessional, or a Priest in a sermon, after the example of our Lord Jesus Christ, His Apostles, and all the Saints, and in accordance with the spirit of the Church, repeatedly insists upon the necessity of prayer, the devil will not be slow to suggest: O, that Superior, that Priest, knows but one rule, but one obligation; he does not care for science, or consider the country and times in which we are living; if you do what he tells, you will never be anything but a real hypocrite and devotee. Should this malignant enemy not succeed by these and similar artifices to prevent certain souls from prayer, he will then try other means. To St. Anthony, the hermit, when at prayer, he would appear in the most hideous forms to frighten him. He would take St. Frances of Rome, shake her and throw her on the ground. When St. Rose of Lima was at prayer, he would come and make a great noise, like taking a basket and jumping about with it. He would often cast large hail-stones upon the two holy Brothers Simplician and Roman, when they knelt down to pray, in order to make them give up prayer, as is related by St. Gregory of Tours.

This implacable hatred and incessant war of Satan against prayer should alone be sufficient to convince you of the necessity, importance, utility and sublimity of this holy exercise, and at the same time urge you on to apply to it with all possible diligence, that you might the sooner acquire the spirit of prayer. Read the life of the seraphic St. Teresa, that great mistress of prayer, and you will find how she struggled for eighteen years to obtain this spirit of prayer. We read of St. Catherine of Bologna, that when she was Abbess, one of her daughters, seeing that her whole time was taken up with business, or by the intercourse she was obliged to have with the servants and strangers, asked her how, with her weak health, she could endure so many fatigues and cares. "Know, my daughter," replied the holy Mother, "and be assured that my mind is so occupied with the things which are not of this world, that at whatever hour or moment I wish, I am immediately united to God and separated from everything bodily and temporal. I confess that this has cost me innumerable sufferings, for the road of virtue is narrow and hard, but, by perseverance, prayer has become my life, my nurse, my mistress, my consolation, my refreshment, my rest, my fortune, all my wealth. It is prayer that has preserved me from mortal sins and rescued me from death ; but it has done more than that ; it has nourished me as a tender mother nourishes her infant with milk. I ought to add, too, that prayer drives away all distractions and temptations, gives us the desire of doing penance, enkindles in us the Divine love, and, finally, that there is no surer road to perfection."

All the Saints, were they to come down from heaven, would, with St. Catherine of Bologna, make the same acknowledgment. The kingdom of heaven suffers violence, and those that use this holy violence will bear it away. Let us, like the Saints, use this salutary violence in regard to ourselves ; it will prove for us a source of joy for all eternity. Let us, in imitation of the Saints, often read a chapter on the great necessity, importance, advantages and efficacy of prayer, thereby to encourage ourselves constantly to persevere and increase in fervor for this holy occupation ; let us be firmly convinced that such a reading will be more profitable to us than any other, whatever it may be. Let us, also, often make our particular examen of conscience on this subject, and let us firmly believe to be true what I one day heard said by a very holy Priest, who was so much given to prayer as to be often elevated in the air whilst in the act of prayer: "Any one," said he, " who would carefully make his particular examen of conscience for half a year, would not fail to attain to contemplation." Suppose the Lord would not favor you in prayer as He has favored certain Saints, yet be convinced you will always receive far more than you deserve; do what you can, and leave to Him to do with you according to His will. "He hath filled the hungry with good things," exclaimed the Blessed Virgin Mary. The Lord not only gives, but overloads with His gifts those who have a real desire for them; join the deed to your desires for them by making use of the means here laid down to acquire them, and rest assured God will deal with you in a most liberal manner, as is peculiar to His Paternal Heart. You will experience what one of my fellow-students has experienced, who said to me one day: "Since I have given myself up to holy prayer, I am quite a different creature." Would to God you had a right heart for all that has been said, and did truly relish it! If you but knew the gift of God you would soon see how sweet the Lord is to those who are given up to prayer. You will most assuredly find Him in this holy exercise, for He opens to those who knock and gives to those that ask. Give it a fair trial. Say with David: "One thing I have asked of the Lord; this will I seek after," (Ps. xxvi. 4,) viz: this gift of prayer, and I will beg and pray for it until it shall be granted to me.

CHAPTER VIII.

EULOGIUM ON PRAYER.

AS there is nothing more necessary or more profitable to man than prayer, the Saints have lavished most profuse eulogies upon this holy exercise. St. John Climachus writes (gradu. 28 initio): "Prayer, considered in its nature or quality, is a familiar conversation and union with God; considered in its efficacy, it is the preservation of the world, the reconciliation with God, the mother of tears, the companion on journeys, the propitiation for sins; a bridge over the high waters of temptation; a bulwark against all assaults of afflictions; the suppression and extinction of wars; the office of the Angels; the nourishment of all souls; the anticipation of future joy; a perpetual occupation, the source of all virtues, the channel of all graces." Not satisfied with these praises, he adds still greater and more important ones: "Prayer is the lever of the spiritual life; the medicine of the soul; the light of the understanding; the expeller of despair; the ground-pillar of Christian hope; the solution of melancholy and sadness; the riches of monks; the treasure of hermits; the cessation of anger; a mirror to show the progress in the spiritual life; the thermometer of the soul; a declaration of the dispositions of the heart; a moral certainty of heavenly glory." To these eulogies on prayer are added (Auct. serm, ad. Fratres in eremo apud St. Aug. serm. 22): "Holy prayer is the column of all virtues; a ladder to God; the support of widows; the foundation of faith; the crown of religious; the sweetness of the married life." To these praises of prayer, St. Augustine adds others: "Prayer is the protection of holy souls; a consolation for the Guardian Angel; an insupportable torment to the devil; a most acceptable homage to God; the best and most perfect praise for penitents and religious; the greatest honor and glory; the preserver of spiritual health." (Aug. ad Probam.) "Prayer," says St. Ephrem, "is the counter-poison of pride; the antidote to the passion of hatred; the best rule in making just laws; the best and most powerful means to govern aright; the standard and trophy in war; a stronghold for peace; the seal of virginity; the guard of nuptial fidelity; the safeguard of travellers; the Guardian Angel during sleep; the source of fertility for the farmer; a safe harbor in the storms of this life; a city of refuge for criminals; the source of all true joy; the best friend and physician of the dying." (Tract de Orat.) "Prayer," says

Cornelius a Lapide, "is the transfiguration of the soul." Prayer, I add, is, moreover, the paradise of the soul ; the Ark of the Covenant ; a wonder-working rod of Moses ; a pillar of cloud by day and a pillar of fire by night ; a Piscina Probatica, or pond of healing-water, wherein whoever descends is healed of whatsoever spiritual infirmity he may lie under ; an impregnable fortress ; the milk of little children ; the crosier of Bishops ; the strength, courage and persuasive power of missionaries ; the conversion of the world ; the Sanctuary of Priests ; the wisdom of the Saints ; the true key of heaven ; the best book of sermons ; the mother of good counsel ; the school of eloquence ; the constancy of the martyrs ; the compass of superiors ; the interpreter of the Holy Scriptures ; the justification for God. If we should say : " I had not sufficient grace to be saved," God will answer : " Why did you not ask it of Me?" the soul-insurance ; an everlasting torment for the damned, seeing how easily they might have been saved by prayer. " Prayer is," says St. John Climachus, " a pious, gentle tyranny towards God, forcing Him to give up to us everything, even Himself." Hence St. Augustine has said with truth : " What can be more excellent than prayer ; what more profitable to our life ; what sweeter to our souls ; what more sublime, in the course of our whole life, than the practice of prayer?"

Being well convinced of this truth, Caspar Sanches, S. J., used to say: "Give me all the goods of the earth, and let them last forever, and I will give them all up for half a quarter of an hour of my usual prayer and communion with God." In like manner said Father Francis Suarez, S. J.: "I am willing to lose all my science rather than one hour of prayer." The saintly Priest of Ars, named Vianney, used to say: "All the happiness of man on earth consists in prayer." One of our Fathers, a holy man of great experience often repeated: "Secular people say, 'in the convent everything is prayer;' but we must reverse their words and say: Prayer is everything to us in the convent." Cornelius a Lapide says: "The gift of prayer is an immense and incomprehensible grace of God." Scarcely did ever any Saint, in fewer words, bestow better praise on prayer than St. Alphonsus, in the preface to his little book on prayer: "I have published several spiritual works, such as Visits to the Blessed Sacrament; Considerations on the Passion of our Lord Jesus Christ; Glories of Mary; a work against the Materialists and Deists, with other devout little treatises; also, a little work on the Infancy of our Saviour, entitled Novena for Christmas; another, called Preparation for death, besides the one on the Eternal Maxims, very useful for meditations or for sermons, to which are added nine discourses, suitable during seasons of divine chastisements. But I am of opinion that I never wrote a more useful book than the present, in which I speak of prayer as a necessary and certain means of obtaining salvation and all the graces which we require for that object. Would to God it were in my power to give a copy of it to every Catholic in the world, to show him the absolute necessity of prayer for salvation."

Such sentiments of the Saints, and of pious souls, proceed from most intimate conviction, and the abundance of the spiritual gifts and graces with which their hearts are overflowing; and it is undoubtedly true that most of men, could they see and comprehend but one-half of the happiness of such souls, would at once give up all earthly pleasures and advantages to enjoy but for one quarter of an hour the happiness of the life of saintly souls. Who, after all this, will remain still cold, careless and indifferent in the practice of prayer? Most assuredly, he only who is *not* of God, and loveth darkness more than light; this world more than his soul; the devil, and all his works and pomps, more than the Lord of heaven and earth.

[The following prayers are so arranged that they can be taken out and put in your prayer-book for daily use.]

PRAYER

TO OBTAIN THE GRACE OF BEING CONSTANT IN PRAYER.

(By St. Alphonsus.)

O GOD of my soul, I hope in Thy goodness that Thou hast pardoned all my offences against Thee, and that I am now in a state of grace. I thank Thee for it with all my heart, and I hope to thank Thee for all eternity: *Misericordias Domini in æternum cantabo.* I know that I have fallen, because I have not had recourse to Thee when I was tempted, to ask for holy perseverance. For the future, I firmly resolve to recommend myself always to Thee, and especially when I see myself in danger of again offending Thee. I will always fly to Thy mercy, invoking always the most holy names of Jesus and Mary, with full confidence that when I pray Thou wilt not fail to give me the strength which I have not of myself to resist my enemies. This I resolve and promise to do. But of what use, O my God, will all these resolutions and promises be, if Thou dost not assist me with Thy grace to put them in practice, that is, to have recourse to Thee in all dangers? Ah, Eternal Father! help me, for the love of Jesus Christ; and let me never omit recommending myself to Thee whenever I am tempted. I know that Thou dost always help me when I have recourse to Thee; but my fear is, that I should forget to recommend myself to Thee, and so my negligence will be the cause of my ruin, that is, the loss of Thy grace, the greatest evil that can happen to me. Ah, by the merits of Jesus Christ, give me grace to pray to Thee; but grant me such an abundant grace that I may always pray, and pray as I ought! O my Mother Mary, whenever I have had recourse to thee, thou hast obtained for me the help which has kept me from falling! Now I come to beg of thee to obtain a still greater grace, namely, that of recommending myself always to thy Son and to thee in all my necessities. My Queen, thou obtainest all thou dost desire from God by the love thou bearest to Jesus Christ; obtain for me now this grace which I beg of thee, namely, to pray always, and never to cease praying till I die. Amen.

PRAYER

TO BE SAID EVERY DAY, TO OBTAIN THE GRACES NECESSARY FOR SALVATION.

(*By St. Alphonsus.*)

ETERNAL Father, Thy Son has promised that Thou wilt grant us all the graces which we ask Thee for in His name. In the name, therefore, and by the merits of Jesus Christ I ask the following graces for myself and for all mankind. And first, I pray Thee to give me a lively faith in all that the holy Roman Church teaches me. Enlighten me also, that I may know the vanity of the goods of this world, and the immensity of the infinite good that Thou art; make me also see the deformity of the sins I have committed, that I may humble myself and detest them as I ought; and, on the other hand, show me how worthy Thou art by reason of Thy goodness, that I should love Thee with all my heart. Make me know also the love Thou hast borne me, that from this day forward I may try to be grateful for so much goodness. Secondly, give me a firm confidence in Thy mercy of receiving the pardon of my sins, holy perseverance, and finally, the glory of paradise, through the merits of Jesus

Christ and the intercession of Mary. Thirdly, give me a great love towards Thee, which shall detach me from the love of this world and of myself, so that I may love none other but Thee, and that I may neither do nor desire anything else but what is for Thy glory. Fourthly, I beg of Thee a perfect resignation to Thy will, in accepting with tranquility sorrows, infirmities, contempt, persecutions, aridity of spirit, loss of property, of esteem, of relations, and every other cross which shall come to me from Thy hands. I offer myself entirely to Thee, that Thou mayest do with me, and all that belongs to me what Thou pleasest; do Thou only give me light and strength to do Thy will; and especially at the hour of death help me to sacrifice my life to Thee with all the affection I am capable of, in union with the sacrifice which Thy Son Jesus Christ made of His life on the Cross on Calvary. Fifthly, I beg of Thee a great sorrow for my sins, which may make me grieve over them as long as I live, and weep for the insults I have offered Thee, the Sovereign Good, who art worthy of infinite love, and who hast loved me so much. Sixthly, I pray Thee to give me the spirit of true humility and meekness, that I may accept with peace, and even with joy, all the contempt, ingratitude and ill-treatment that I may receive. At the same time I also pray Thee to give me perfect charity, which shall make me wish well to those who have done evil to me, and to do what good I can, at least by praying, for those who have in any way injured me. Seventhly, I beg of Thee to give me a love for the virtue of holy mortification, by which I may chastise my rebellious senses, and cross my self-love; at the same time, I beg Thee to give me holy purity of body and the grace to resist all bad temptations, by ever having recourse to Thee and Thy most holy Mother. Give me grace faithfully to obey my spiritual father and all my superiors in all things. Give me an upright intention, that in all I desire and do I may seek only Thy glory, and to please Thee alone. Give me a great confidence in the Passion of Jesus Christ, and in the intercession of Mary immaculate. Give me a great love towards the most Adorable Sacrament of the Altar, and a tender devotion and love to Thy holy Mother. Give me, I pray thee, above all, holy perseverance, and the grace always to pray for it, especially in time of temptation and at the hour of death.

Lastly, I recommend to Thee the holy souls of Purgatory, my relations and benefactors; and in an especial manner I recommend to Thee all those who hate me or who have in any way offended me; I beg of Thee to render them good for the evil they have done, or may wish to do me. Finally, I recommend to Thee all infidels, heretics, and all poor sinners; give them light and strength to deliver themselves from sin. Oh, most loving God, make Thyself known and loved by all, but especially by those who have been more ungrateful to Thee than others, so that by thy goodness I may come one day to sing Thy mercies in Paradise ; for my hope is in the merits of Thy blood, and in the patronage of Mary. O Mary, Mother of God, pray to Jesus for me ! So I hope ; so may it be !

PRAYER OF CHLODWIG, (CLOVIS),

HEATHEN KING OF THE FRANKS, WHEN WITH HIS WHOLE ARMY IN IMMINENT DANGER OF BEING DEFEATED BY THE ALEMANNI.

" JESUS CHRIST, Thou of Whom Chlotilde (the king's Christian wife) has often told me that Thou art the Son of the living God, and that Thou givest aid to the hard-pressed and victory to those who trust in Thee, I humbly crave Thy powerful assistance. If Thou grantest me the victory over my enemies I will believe in Thee and be baptized in Thy name. For I have called upon my gods in vain. They must be impotent, as they cannot help those who serve them. Now I invoke Thee, desiring to believe in Thee ; do, then, deliver me from the hands of my adversaries."

No sooner had Chlodwig uttered this prayer than the Alemanni became panic-stricken, took to flight, and soon after, seeing their king slain, sued for peace. Thereupon Chlodwig blended both nations, the Franks and the Alemanni together—returned home and became a Christian. Should any one of my readers be still groping in the darkness of unbelief or error, I would kindly request him to pray in the same spirit, adapting King Chlodwig's prayer to his own circumstances, or to say the prayer which F. Thayer, a minister of the Anglican Church, used to say when he was yet in doubt and uncertainty, and by the use of which he obtained for himself the gift of faith.

F. THAYER'S PRAYER

FOR GUIDANCE INTO TRUTH.

GOD of all goodness, almighty and eternal Father of mercies, and Saviour of mankind; I implore Thee, by Thy sovereign goodness, to enlighten my mind and to touch my heart, that, by means of true faith, hope, and charity, I may live and die in the true religion of Jesus Christ. I confidently believe that, as there is but one God, there can be but one faith, one religion, one only path to salvation, and that every other path opposed thereto can lead but to perdition. This path, O my God, I anxiously seek after, that I may follow it, and be saved. Therefore I protest before Thy Divine Majesty, and I swear by all Thy divine attributes, that I will follow the religion which Thou shalt reveal to me as the true one, and will abandon, at whatever cost, that wherein I shall have discovered errors and falsehood. I confess that I do not deserve this favor for the greatness of my sins, for which I am truly penitent, seeing they offend a God Who is so good, so holy, and so worthy of love; but what I deserve not I hope to obtain from Thine infinite mercy; and I beseech Thee to grant it unto me through the merits of that precious Blood, which was shed for us sinners by Thine only Son, Jesus Christ our Lord, Who liveth and reigneth, &c. Amen.

Truly, such a sincere and humble prayer will not remain unheard.

EJACULATION.

My Lord Jesus Christ, for the sake of Thy sufferings, grant me such faith, hope, charity, sorrow for my sins, and love for prayer, as will save and sanctify my soul.

[It would be well to repeat this ejaculation often in the course of the day.]

www.ingramcontent.com/pod-product-compliance
Lightning Source LLC
Chambersburg PA
CBHW032008230426
43672CB00010B/2293